BUTTERICK'S 1892
METROPOLITAN FASHIONS

BUTTERICK'S 1892 METROPOLITAN FASHIONS

The Butterick Publishing Co.

DOVER PUBLICATIONS, INC.
New York

Bibliographical Note

This Dover edition, first published in 1994, is a new selection of material from *Metropolitan Fashions For Autumn and Winter, 1892–'93, Vol. XXXVI, No. 1*, published by The Butterick Publishing Co. (Limited), London and New York, n.d. [1892]. A new Introduction has been written for this edition.

Library of Congress Cataloging-in-Publication Data

Butterick's 1892 metropolitan fashions / Butterick Publishing Co.
      p.   cm.
   Reprint. Originally published under title: Metropolitan fashions for autumn and winter, 1892–1893. London : Butterick, 1892.
   ISBN 0-486-27983-9
   1. Dressmaking—Patterns—Catalogs. 2. Tailoring—Patterns—Catalogs. 3. Costume—United States—History—19th century. I.Butterick Publishing Company.
TT520.B96 1994
646.4′07—dc20   94-13379
                                                                        CIP

Manufactured in the United States of America
Dover Publications, Inc., 31 East 2nd Street, Mineola, N.Y. 11501

INTRODUCTION

HOME SEWING, originally a matter of necessity, has become today a creative outlet for many women. For most contemporary home sewers this begins with two initial steps—the selection of a fabric and a trip to the pattern counter. The pattern chosen will then serve as a guide, from the first snip of the scissors to the last stitch of the hem. Even a neophyte dressmaker, if she follows a modern pattern and the directions that come with it, can turn out a reasonably successful garment.

Brought up in a ready-to-wear world where home sewing is the exception rather than the rule, it is hard for most of us to realize that until well into the twentieth century, most clothes were made at home, and before the middle of the nineteenth century, everything had to be sewn entirely by hand. Those who could afford to do so, and the number was not very large, had their clothes made by a tailor or dressmaker; the rest had to rely on the skills of their women at home. Both professionals and amateurs did their best to interpret the fashions of their day by referring to available fashion plates or to what they admired in the apparel of others. Patterns, as we know them, did not exist then. Judging from surviving costumes, there was a high degree of artistry and competence, but the amount of time it must have taken to produce them precludes the possibility of any wide-range production, and one may assume that these were one of a kind and in limited supply.

Two developments in sequence—the sewing machine and the graded pattern—were to revolutionize the making of clothes. European inventors had been working to perfect a machine which would stitch as early as the 1790s, but their efforts were either ignored or sabotaged by tailors who were fearful of being displaced by such an apparatus. It was not until 1846, after Elias Howe, an American, applied for and was granted a patent, that sewing machines became a practical reality. By the late 1850s, they were produced in quantity and could be purchased for about $50.00.

Although this was a monumental boon to dressmakers and home sewers, it did not solve all their problems. In the 1860s, fashions were becoming increasingly complicated, and even though the sewing machine could put seams together quickly, it was still up to the sewer to figure out how the garment should be made. To produce a gown of the latest fashion and one that would also fit the wearer called for careful planning, skillful cutting and, at times, lucky guesswork.

In 1863, Ebenezer Butterick, a tailor, and his wife, after some years of experimentation, introduced the paper pattern with graded sizes. Originally designed for boys' shirts, its potential was immediately recognized. Very shortly afterwards, graded patterns for women's and children's garments were available as well. This enterprise was so successful that in 1871 the Buttericks sold over 6,000,000 patterns, despite the fact that other companies had now entered the field. Ebenezer Butterick went on to publish *Metropolitan Fashions*, a catalog of patterns "representing every variety of wear from swaddling clothes of the nursery kind to the elaborate costumes of society Belle." It is interesting to note at this point that "every variety of wear" included little men's wear. Except for such items as shirts, some underwear and nightwear, relatively few clothes for men were included in pattern books.

Here we present a selection of fashions from a rare 1892–1893 issue of *Metropolitan Fashions*. The magazine consisted of a basic catalog of all the patterns the company manufactured, plus monthly supplements presenting new patterns. The magazine is too large to make it feasible to present all of the patterns, but we have included as many patterns from the July–December supplements, together with the original captions, as possible.

Most of the fashions were shown more than once, often combined with other patterns, or in different fabrics. Many of the original captions, therefore, contain cross references to other pages. Because we have had to rearrange the drawings in order to fit them onto our page size, these page references are no longer accurate.

In 1892, mass production of clothing was as yet in its infancy. Most wearing apparel was still made at home. The rudiments of the ready-to-wear industry, however, were already there, and these illustrations of patterns reflect growing standardization. Although subscribers were given some choice, the initial selection was made for them. Editors would go through magazines, attend or read about important social events, interview or study reports on Paris and New York couturiers, etc., for fashion ideas. Their information would be turned over to the technicians and, after consultation, the designs would be copied, altered or modified for popular consumption. These would then be translated into patterns. The suggested fashions ranged from those requiring both a sizable income and an experienced dressmaker to reproduce, to some fashions that called for inexpensive fabric and were fairly simple to make.

Although Parisian fashions of 1892 were well on the way toward the "hourglass" silhouette of the mid-'90s, the fashions illustrated in this pattern book reflect a certain "provincial lag" and still bear a strong resemblance to the styles of the late 1880s. Most of them show vestiges of the bustle back, and some of the skirts included have the draped fronts popular during the preceding decade (pp. 129, 136). Even the petticoats were designed with extra back fullness (pp. 71, 137). The new interest in sleeves, however, had been picked up and featured (pp. 17, 31, 45, 70, 77, 112, 116). Necklines are generally high. Some latitude was allowed in evening wear, but the low decolletage for evening, which was to become so fashionable later, is as yet hardly perceptible.

By this time a degree of masculinity had begun to creep into women's fashions, particularly in the jackets and coats. Eton (pp. 28, 35, 110), Hussar (pp. 30, 35) and Norfolk (pp. 40, 49, 56, 65) jackets, blazers (p. 32), reefers (p. 59) and coats with military capes (p. 106) all show strong masculine influence. Many pages of the journal are devoted to these jackets, as well as to skirts and blouses. Both popular and fashionable by then, these separates, when mixed and matched, permitted even those with limited wardrobes to appear well dressed.

Patterns for underwear, which for the most part was still sewn at home, are also included. Made of cotton or linen, always white, drawers, chemises, nightwear, etc. varied from simple to fussy in design. The wrappers, such as those that appear on pages 12, 20, 35, 38, 83 and 118, probably double as maternity gowns.

Except for the length of the skirts, fashions for girls were similar to those of their mothers. Very young girls wore their skirts at mid-calf length; young ladies (up to about age 16) wore them ankle length. Unlike today, clothes for boys had some feminine aspects. Their costumes consisted mainly of knee-length pants and blouses, whereas very small boys wore skirts (pp. 40, 54, 58, 66). On pages 41 and 69 are illustrations of the famous "Lord Fauntleroy" suit.

Concentrating on women and children, *Metropolitan Fashions* overlooked neither the great events of life such as weddings and funerals, including both a bridal costume (p. 41) and a mourning toilette (p. 133), nor the small moments, offering patterns for dolls' clothes and a variety of accessories.

This was still a period when one dressed for the time of day, the occasion and the activity; many of the garments illustrated are so identified. Most books on costume history touch only on the high points of a period. The rich variety included in this volume, the carefully detailed engravings and the explicit captions not only provide a rare opportunity to examine in some depth fashions as they were presented to millions of Americans in 1892, but also to learn from these fashions something of the modes and manners of our country at that time.

STELLA BLUM

4577

No. 4577. — LADIES' CAPE-COLLARS (To be Made Up as Two, Three or Four Cape-Collars) (Copyr't). — These collars may be again seen at figure No. 284 A on page 74. In the present instance cloth was chosen for making them, and fancy braid provides a tasteful trimming. Such a garment may be worn as a shoulder wrap or as an accessory to a top garment, and may be made of any desired fabric. The pattern is in 5 sizes for ladies from 30 to 46 inches, bust measure. For a lady of medium size, the collars require 1⅝ yard of material 44 inches wide, or 1½ yard of goods 50 inches wide. Price of pattern, 7d. or 15 cents.

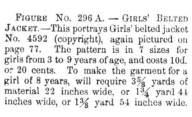

4577

4610

FIGURE No. 296 A. — GIRLS' BELTED JACKET.—This portrays Girls' belted jacket No. 4592 (copyright), again pictured on page 77. The pattern is in 7 sizes for girls from 3 to 9 years of age, and costs 10d. or 20 cents. To make the garment for a girl of 8 years, will require 3⅝ yards of material 22 inches wide, or 1¾ yard 44 inches wide, or 1⅜ yard 54 inches wide.

4610

No. 4610.—LADIES' RUSSIAN BASQUE (Copyright).— At figure No. 262 A on page 77 this basque is shown differently developed. Serge was chosen for the blouse in the present instance, and gimp and feather bands comprise the garniture. The pattern is in 13 sizes for ladies from 28 to 46 inches, bust measure To make the basque for a lady of medium size, will require 5¾ yards of material 22 inches wide, or 4½ yards 30 inches wide, or 3⅛ yards 44 inches wide. If goods 50 inches wide be selected, then 2⅝ yards will prove sufficient. Price of pattern, 1s. 3d or 30 cents.

4610

FIGURE No. 263 A.—LADIES' RUSSIAN TOILETTE.—This consists of Ladies' Russian blouse-waist No. 4600 (copyright), and Russian skirt No. 4603 (copyright), both shown on page 74. The skirt pattern is in 9 sizes for ladies from 20 to 36 inches, waist measure, and costs 1s. 6d. or 35 cts. The waist is in 13 sizes for ladies from 28 to 46 inches, bust measure, and costs 1s. or 25 cts. For goods needed, see page 74.

No. 4578.—Misses' and Girls' Cape-Collars (To be Made up as Two, Three or Four Cape-Collars) (Copyright).—At figure No. 292 A on this page these collars may be again seen. Mode cloth was chosen for them in this instance, with silk braid for trimming. Dress goods and light-weight cloakings are appropriate for this garment, and the edges may be pinked or edged with gimp or braid. The pattern is in 7 sizes from 4 to 16 years of age. To make the collars for a miss of 12 years, needs 2 yards of goods 22 inches wide, or 1⅜ yard either 44 or 54 inches wide. Price of pattern, 5d. or 10 cents.

4578

4578

4578

4615

4615

Figure No. 294 A.—Misses' Russian Toilette.—This consists of Misses' Russian waist No. 4583 (copyright), and Russian skirt No. 4602 (copyright), both shown again on page 76. For the sizes, prices and quantities of goods needed, see the page just mentioned.

No. 4615.—Ladies' Cape, with Yoke (To be made with One, Two or Three Upper Capes) (Copyright).—At figure No. 272 A on page 73 another view of this cape may be observed. The pattern is in 10 sizes for ladies from 28 to 46 inches, bust measure. To make the garment for a lady of medium size, needs 6 yards of material 44 inches wide, or 4¾ yards 50 or 54 inches wide. Price of pattern, 1s. 6d. or 35 cents.

Figure No. 270 A.—Ladies' Corselet Princess Costume.—This represents Ladies' corselet Princess costume No. 4614 (copyright), pictured again on page 78. The pattern is in 13 sizes for ladies from 28 to 46 inches, bust measure, and costs 1s. 8d. or 40 cents. To make the costume of one material for a lady of medium size, requires 10⅞ yards 22 inches wide, or 5⅝ yards 44 inches wide, or 5 yards 50 inches wide. In the combination illustrated on page 78, it needs 4⅜ yards of shot suiting 40 inches wide, with 4½ yards of plain silk 20 inches wide.

6

FIGURE NO. 292 A.—GIRLS' CAPE-COLLARS.—This depicts Girls' cape-collars No. 4578 (copyright), which are again represented on this page. The pattern is developed in sizes which also adapt it to misses' wear. It is in 7 sizes from 4 to 16 years of age, and costs 5d. or 10 cents. To make the garment for a miss of 12 years, will require 2 yards of material 22 inches wide, or 1⅜ yard 44 inches wide. Of goods 54 inches wide, 1⅜ yard will suffice.

4595   **4595**

NO. 4595.—INFANTS' DRESS, WITH SEAMLESS YOKE (Copyright).—The pattern is in one size, and, for a garment like it, will require 2½ yards of any suitable goods 36 inches wide. Price of pattern, 10d. or 20 cents.

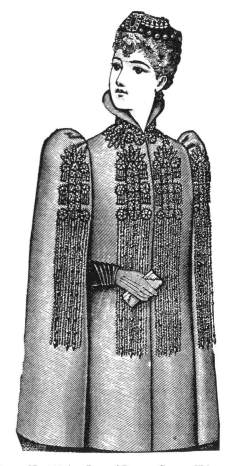

FIGURE NO. 283 A.—LADIES' REEFER CAPE.—This illustrates Ladies' cape No. 4575 (copyright), which is shown again on this page. The pattern is in 11 sizes for ladies from 28 to 48 inches, bust measure, and costs 1s. or 25 cents. To make the garment for a lady of medium size, will require 3⅞ yards of material 22 inches wide, or 2½ yards 44 inches wide, or 1⅞ yard 54 inches wide.

FIGURE NO. 297 A. — GIRLS' RUSSIAN DRESS. — This pictures Girls' Russian dress No. 4580 (copyright), which is again shown on page 77 of this publication. The pattern is in 11 sizes for girls from 2 to 12 years of age, and costs 10d. or 20 cents. Of one material for a girl of 8 years, the dress requires 5⅛ yards 22 inches wide, or 4 yards 30 inches wide. Of goods 44 inches wide, 2⅝ yards will be sufficient.

FIGURE NO. 287 A.— GIRLS' DRESS.— This is Girls' dress No. 4608 (copyright), also pictured on page 74. The pattern is in 8 sizes for girls from 5 to 12 years of age, and costs 1s. or 25 cents. For a girl of 8 years, it needs 5⅛ yards of material 22 inches wide, or 3¾ yards 30 inches wide, or 2½ yards 44 inches wide.

4616   **4616**

NO. 4616.—CHILD'S COAT, SHIRRED IN YOKE OUTLINE (Copyright). — The pattern of this coat is in 7 sizes for children from ½ to 6 years old. For a child of 5 years, it needs 4⅝ yards of goods 22 inches wide, or 2¼ yards 44 inches wide, or 2¼ yards 54 ins. wide. Price of pattern, 10d. or 20 cts.

No. 4609.--Little Girls' Dress (Copyr't).—This dainty little dress will be appropriate for woollen and cotton fabrics, and the decoration may be as simple or elaborate as desired. The pattern is in 7 sizes for little girls from ½ to 6 years of age. For a girl of 5 years, it needs 5⅝ yards of material 22 inches wide, or 3¾ yds. 36 inches wide. If goods 44 inches wide be chosen, then 2⅞ yards will suffice. Price of pattern, 10d. or 20 cents.

4609

4609

4612

4612

No. 4612.—Misses' Russian Blouse (With Fitted Linings) (Copyright).—This blouse is again shown at figure No. 293 A on page 76 of this issue. The pattern is in 7 sizes for misses from 10 to 16 years of age, and will make up attractively in any variety of dress goods. To make the blouse for a miss of 12 years, will require 4⅞ yards of goods 22 inches wide, or 3⅞ yards 30 inches wide, or 2⅜ yards 44 inches wide, or 2⅜ yards 50 inches wide. Price of pattern, 1s. or 25 cts.

4575

4575

4575

4575

Figure No. 272 A.—Ladies' Visiting Toilette.—This consists of Ladies' cape No. 4615 (copyright), shown on page 72; and skirt No. 4526 (copyright), seen on page 34. For sizes, prices and goods needed, see pages 34 and 72.

No. 4575.—Ladies' Reefer Cape (Copyright).—This stylish cape may be seen differently developed at figure No. 283 A on this page. It is here shown made of plain cloth and decorated with feather trimming and a handsome braiding design. The garment may be made up with the center seam closed to the edge or terminated a short distance below the waist-line, both styles being clearly shown in the engravings. The pattern is in 11 sizes for ladies from 28 to 48 inches, bust measure. For a lady of medium size, it needs 3⅞ yards of goods 22 inches wide, or 2½ yards 44 inches wide, or 1⅞ yard 54 inches wide. Price of pattern, 1s. or 25 cents.

Figure No. 291 A.—Girls' Toilette.—This consists of Girls' skirt No. 4375 (copyright), pictured on page 54; and blouse No 4596 (copyright), shown on page 78. The skirt pattern is in 13 sizes from 4 to 16 years of age, and costs 1s. or 25 cents. The blouse pattern is in 9 sizes from 8 to 16 years old, and costs 1s. or 25 cents. For a girl of 12 years, they need 8⅝ yards of goods 22 inches wide.

4605

4605   **4605**

No. 4605.—LADIES' COAT (Copyright).—This coat is shown again at figure No. 280 A on this page. The collar may be rolled slightly or quite deeply, as preferred. Tan or mode melton will make a handsome coat of this kind, and large pearl buttons and machine-stitching will form a suitable finish. The pattern is in 13 sizes for ladies from 28 to 46 inches, bust measure. To make the coat for a lady of medium size, will require 5 yards of material 22 inches wide, or 2½ yards 44 inches wide. If 54-inch-wide goods be used, 2 yards will suffice. Price of pattern, 1s. 3d. or 30 cents.

4584

4584

4584   **4584**

FIGURE No. 280 A.—LADIES' STREET TOILETTE.—This consists of Ladies' coat No. 4605 (copyr't), shown again on this page; and Watteau skirt No. 4564 (copyr't), on page **34.** The coat pattern is 13 sizes for ladies from 28 to 46 inches, bust measure. and costs 1s. 3d. or 30 cts. The **skirt** pattern is in 9 sizes for ladies from 20 to 36 inches, **waist** measure. and costs 1s. 6d. or 35 cts. For a lady of **medium** size, they need 11⅛ yds. of goods 22 ins. wide.

No. 4584.—LADIES' GREEK COSTUME, WITH TRAIN (PER-FORATED FOR ROUND LENGTH) (KNOWN AS THE HYPATIA GOWN) (Copyright).—This pattern, shown again at figure No. 276 A on page 76, is in 12 sizes for ladies from 28 to 46 inches, bust measure. For a lady of medium size, the costume requires 11⅞ yards of goods 22 inches wide, or 6⅜ yards 44 inches wide, or 5⅞ yards 50 inches wide. Price of pattern, 1s. 8d. or 40 cents.

9

4599

4599

4599

4600

4600

No. 4599. — Misses' Rus-
sian Blouse-Waist (Copy-
right).––This pattern, which
is shown again at figure No.
No. 289 A on page 75, is in
7 sizes for misses from 10 to
16 years of age. To make
the garment for a miss of 12
years. will require 3⅜ yards
of material 22 inches wide, or
2⅝ yards 30 inches wide. or
1⅞ yard 44 inches wide.
Price of pattern, 10d. or 20 cts.

No. 4600. — Ladies' Russian
Blouse-Waist (Copyright). — This
garment may be again seen at figure No. 263 A on page 72. The
pattern is in 13 sizes for ladies from
28 to 46 inches, bust measure. To
make the blouse-waist for a lady of
medium size, will require 4¼ yards
of material 22 inches wide, or 3¼
yards 30 inches wide, or 2⅜ yards 44
inches wide. If material 50 inches
wide be used. then 2 yards will suffice. Price of pattern, 1s. or 25 cents.

4600

4582

4582

4582

No. 4582.—Ladies' Russian Skirt, with a Slight Train (Perforated for Round
Length) (Copyright).—This stylishly devised skirt may be again observed by referring to
figures Nos. 273 A and 282 A on pages 75 and 76 of this publication. The pattern is in
9 sizes for ladies from 20 to 36 inches, waist measure. To make the skirt of one material
for a lady of medium size, will require 6⅜ yards 22 inches wide, or 5 yards 30 inches wide,
or 3⅝ yards 44 inches wide, or 3⅝ yards 50 inches wide. Price of pattern, 1s. 6d. or 35 cents.

Figure No. 277 A.—Ladies' Morning Toilette.—This consists of Ladies' dressing-
sack No. 4611 (copyright), which is shown on page 78 of this publication; and bell petticoat No. 4523 (copyright), also represented on page 39. The sack pattern is in 13 sizes
for ladies from 28 to 46 inches, bust measure, and costs 1s. or 25 cents. The petticoat
pattern is in 9 sizes for ladies from 20 to 36 inches, waist measure, and costs 1s. or 25
cents. To make the toilette for a lady of medium size, will require 9⅜ yards of material 22 inches wide; the sack calling for 4 yards, and the petticoat for 5⅜ yards.

4589

4608   **4608**

No. 4608.—Girls' Dress (Copyright). — Another illustration of this dress is given at figure No. 287 A on page 72 of this issue. The pattern is in 8 sizes for girls from 5 to 12 years of age. To make the dress of one material for a girl of 8 years, needs 5⅛ yards 22 inches wide, or 3¾ yards 30 inches wide, or 2½ yards 44 inches wide. Price of pattern, 1s. or 25 cents.

4589

4589

4589

4589

Figure No. 259 A.—Ladies' Street Toilette.—This consists of Ladies' cape No. 4589 (copyright), shown again on this page; and skirt No. 4482 (copyright), seen on page 35. The cape pattern is in 10 sizes for ladies from 28 to 46 inches, bust measure, and costs 1s. 3d. or 30 cents. The skirt pattern is in 9 sizes for ladies from 20 to 36 inches, waist measure, and costs 1s. 6d. or 35 cents. Of goods 44 inches wide for a lady of medium size, the cape needs 4⅝ yards, and the skirt 3⅛ yards.

No. 4589.—Ladies' Cape (To be Made with One, Two or Three Flounces) (Copyright).— This pattern, shown again at figure No. 259 A on this page, is in 10 sizes for ladies from 28 to 46 inches, bust measure. In the combination pictured for a lady of medium size, it requires 1⅜ yard of cloth 54 inches wide for the collar and cape, with 2⅛ yards of flouncing 14¾ inches wide for the upper flounce, 2½ yards of flouncing 14¾ inches wide for the middle flounce, and 3 yards of flouncing 14¾ inches wide for the lowest flounce. Of one material, it needs 8⅜ yards 22 inches wide, or 4⅝ yards 44 ins. wide. Price of pattern, 1s. 3d. or 30 cts.

Figure No. 295 A.—Girls' Toilette.—This consists of Girls' dress No. 4594 (copyright), seen on page 77; and guimpe No. 4478 (copyright), on page 52. The dress pattern is in 8 sizes for girls from 5 to 12 years old, and costs 1s. or 25 cents. The guimpe pattern is in 11 sizes for girls from 2 to 12 years old, and costs 5d or 10 cents. For a girl of 8 years, the toilette needs 8¼ yards of material 22 inches wide.

FIGURE NO. 284 A.—LADIES' TOIL-
ETTE.—This consists of Ladies' cape-
collars No. 4577 (copyright), pictured
on page 72; corselet with suspenders
No. 4551 (copyright), on page 13; and
blouse No. 3551 (copyright). on its label.
For sizes, prices, and quantities of goods
needed, see pages mentioned above.

4591

4591

4591

NO. 4591.—
LADIES' TUNIC
OR SLEEVELESS
JACKET, OPEN IN
THE BACK (TO BE
WORN WITH OR
WITHOUT A BELT)
(Copyright).— At
figures Nos. 267 A
and 266 A on
pages 75 and
78, this tunic is
again illustrated.
The pattern is in
7 sizes for ladies
from 28 to 40
inches, bust
measure. To
make the garment
for a lady of me-
dium size, will
require 5 yards
of goods 22 in-
ches wide, or 2⅞
yards 44 inches
wide, or 2⅛ yards
50 inches wide.
Price of pattern,
1s. 3d. or 30 cents.

4606

4606

FIGURE NO. 267 A.—LA-
DIES' TOILETTE.—This con-
sists of Ladies' tunic No.
4591 (copyright), shown on
page 74; and basque No.
4570 (copyright), seen on
page 32. The tunic pattern
is in 7 sizes for ladies from
28 to 40 inches, bust measure, and costs 1s. 3d. or 30
cents. The basque pattern
is in 13 sizes for ladies from
28 to 46 inches, bust measure, and costs 1s. 3d. or 30
cents. Of one material for
a lady of medium size, the
toilette requires 10 yards
22 inches wide; the tunic
calling for 5 yards, and the
basque for 5 yards. If goods
44 inches wide be used,
then 5½ yards will suffice.

NO. 4606.—LADIES' YOKE WRAPPER OR LOUNGING-ROBE (Copyright).—Another view
of this comfortable wrapper is given at figure No. 271 A on page 77 of this publication.
The garment is here shown made of Surah, with a ruching of the material and ribbon bows
for garniture. The pattern is in 13 sizes for ladies from 28 to 46 inches, bust measure.
For a lady of medium size, it requires 10⅜ yards of material 22 inches wide, or 7½ yards
30 inches wide, or 5⅜ yards 44 inches wide. Price of pattern, 1s. 6d. or 35 cents.

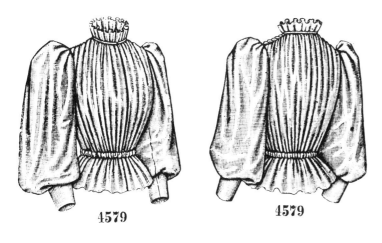

4579   4579

No. 4579.—MISSES' GUIMPE (Copyright).—White mull was chosen for making this simple guimpe. The pattern is in 7 sizes for misses from 10 to 16 years of age. To make the guimpe for a miss of 12 years, requires 5¼ yards of material 22 inches wide, or 4 yards 27 inches wide, or 3¾ yards 36 inches wide, or 3⅛ yards 44 inches wide. Price of pattern, 7d. or 15 cents.

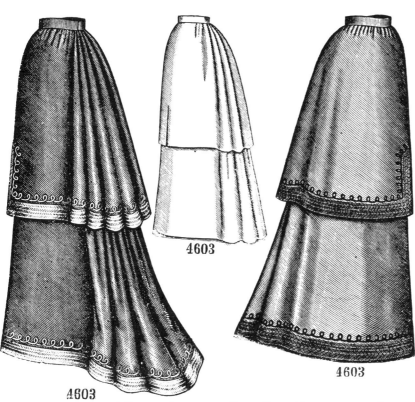

4603

4603   4603

No. 4603.—LADIES' RUSSIAN SKIRT, WITH SHORT TRAIN (PERFORATED FOR ROUND LENGTH) (Copyright).—At figure No. 263 A on page 72, this skirt is also shown. French serge is here represented, and Hercules and soutache braid forms the garniture. The pattern is in 9 sizes for ladies from 20 to 36 inches, waist measure. For a lady of medium size, it requires 7⅜ yards of material 22 inches wide, or 5⅝ yards 30 inches wide, or 4 yards 44 inches wide, or 3¼ yards 50 inches wide. Price of pattern, 1s. 6d. or 35 cents.

4607   4607

No. 4607.—MISSES' RUSSIAN BLOUSE (WITH FITTED LININGS) (Copyright).—This pattern, shown again at figure No. 285 A on page 77. is in 7 sizes for misses from 10 to 16 years old. For a miss of 12 years. it calls for 4½ yards of goods 22 inches wide, or 3¼ yards 30 inches wide, or 2⅜ yards 44 inches wide, or 2¼ yards 50 inches wide. Price of pattern, 1s. or 25 cents.

FIGURE No. 273 A.—LADIES' VISITING TOILETTE.—This consists of Ladies' Watteau cape No. 4585 (copyr't), shown on page 78; and Russian skirt No. 4582 (copyr't), on page 73. For sizes, prices, and goods needed, see pages 73 and 78.

13

No. 4576.—Misses' Five-Gored Bell Skirt (Copyright).— By referring to figures Nos. 288 A and 285 A on pages 75 and 77, this stylish skirt may again be observed. All kinds of seasonable woollens will make up well in this way, and any preferred foot trimming may be added. The pattern is in 7 sizes for misses from 10 to 16 years of age. To make the skirt for a miss of 12 years, will require $4\frac{1}{8}$ yards of material 22 inches wide, or $3\frac{1}{8}$ yards 30 inches wide, or 2 yards 44 inches wide, or $1\frac{5}{8}$ yard 50 inches wide. Price of pattern, 1s. 3d. or 30 cents.

4576

4576

Figure No. 300 A.—Little Girls' Dress.— This illustrates Little Girls' dress No. 4586 (copyright), shown on page 76. The pattern is in 7 sizes for little girls from 1 to 7 years old, and costs 10d. or 20 cents. For a girl of 5 years, it needs $4\frac{1}{2}$ yards of goods 22 inches wide.

Figure No. 288 A.—Misses' Toilette —This consists of Misses' blouse No. 4581 (copyright), which is differently pictured on page 78 of this issue; and bell skirt No. 4576 (copyr't), shown again on this page. Gray flannel was here used for the toilette, and fancy braid provides the trimming. The blouse pattern is in 9 sizes for misses from 8 to 16 years of age, and costs 1s. or 25 cents. The skirt pattern is in 7 sizes for misses from 10 to 16 years of age, and costs 1s. 3d. or 30 cents. For a miss of 12 years, the toilette requires $8\frac{3}{8}$ yards of material 22 inches wide; the blouse calling for $4\frac{1}{4}$ yards, and the skirt for $4\frac{1}{8}$ yards. Of goods 44 inches wide, $4\frac{1}{8}$ yards will suffice: the blouse needing $2\frac{1}{8}$ yards; and the skirt, 2 yards.

Figure No. 268 A.—Ladies' Russian Costume.— This portrays Ladies' costume No. 4613 (copyright), seen on page 77. The pattern is in 13 sizes for ladies from 28 to 46 inches, bust measure, and costs 1s. 8d. or 40 cents. Of one material for a lady of medium size, it needs 13 yards 22 inches wide.

4590

4590

No.4590.—Ladies' Tunic or Sleeveless Jacket (Copyright).—This tunic receives further illustration at figure No. 275 A on this page and at figure No. 274 A on page 77. Old-blue cloth was used for the garment in this instance, and feather trimming provides the ornamentation. The pattern is in 7 sizes for ladies from 28 to 40 inches, bust measure. For a lady of medium size, it calls for 4½ yards of material 22 inches wide, or 3⅜ yards 44 inches wide, or 2½ yards 50 inches wide. Price of pattern, 1s. 3d. or 30 cents.

Figure No. 289 A.—Misses' Russian Toilette.—This consists of Misses' Russian blouse-waist No. 4599 (copyr't), shown on page 73; and Russian skirt No. 4602 (copyr't), on page 76. For prices, sizes, and quantities of goods needed, refer to the pages just mentioned.

Figure No. 275 A.—Ladies' Promenade Toilette.—This consists of Ladies' tunic No. 4590 (copyr't), which is again pictured on this page; and costume No. 4571 (copyright), shown on page 16. The costume pattern is in 13 sizes for ladies from 28 to 46 inches, bust measure, and costs 1s. 8d. or 40 cents. The tunic pattern is in 7 sizes for ladies from 28 to 40 inches, bust measure, and costs 1s. 3d. or 30 cents. For a lady of medium size, they need 15⅛ yards of material 22 inches wide: the costume requiring 10⅝ yards; and the tunic, 4½ yards.

4586

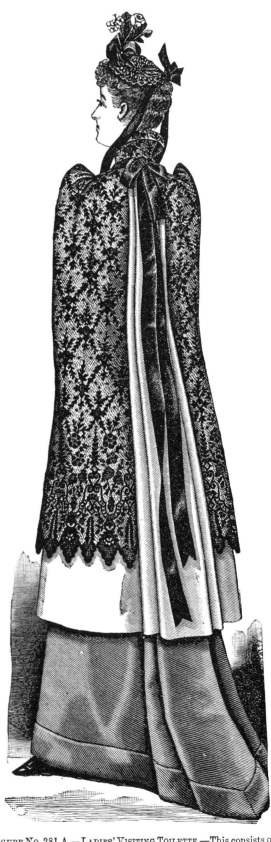

4586

No. 4586.—LITTLE GIRLS'
DRESS (Copyr't).—At figure
No. 300 A on page 75 this
dress is again seen. Challis
showing tiny sprays of blue
flowers on a cream ground
was here used for the dress,
and blue baby ribbon trims
it. The pattern is in 7 sizes
for little girls from 1 to 7
years of age, and will make
up nicely in any pliable
material, such as cashmere,
India, China or wash silk,
etc. To make the dress for
a girl of 5 years, will need
4½ yards of goods 22
inches wide, or 3½ yards
30 inches wide, or 2⅜ yards
44 inches wide. Price
of pattern, 10d. or 20 cents.

FIGURE No. 276 A.— LADIES' GREEK COSTUME.—This
portrays Ladies' Greek costume No. 4584 (copyr't), again
seen on page 73. The pattern is in 12 sizes for ladies
from 28 to 44 inches, bust measure, and costs 1s. 8d. or
40 cents. For a lady of medium size, it needs 11⅞ yards
of goods 22 inches wide, or 6⅜ yards 44 inches wide.

FIGURE No. 281 A.—LADIES' VISITING TOILETTE.—This consists of
Ladies' cape No. 4597 (copyright), again shown on page 77; and
skirt No. 4564 (copyright), seen on page 34. The cape pattern is
in 10 sizes for ladies from 28 to 46 inches, bust measure, and costs
1s. 6d. or 35 cents. The skirt pattern is in 9 sizes for ladies from
20 to 36 inches, waist measure, and costs 1s. 6d. or 35 cents. For a
lady of medium size, they need 8¾ yards of goods 44 inches wide.

No. 4588.—LADIES' BISHOP DRESS SLEEVE (Copyr't).—This sleeve is shown developed in plain dress goods and plainly finished. The pattern is in 7 sizes for ladies from 9 to 15 inches, arm measure, measuring about an inch below the bottom of the arm's-eye. To make a pair of sleeves for a lady whose arm measures 11 inches as described, will need 2⅜ yards of goods 22 inches wide, or 1¾ yard 27 inches wide, or 1⅝ yard 36 inches wide, or 1⅝ yard 44 inches wide. Price of pattern, 5d. or 10 cents.

4588

4574

4574

No. 4574.—MISSES' APRON (Copyright).—This pattern, also shown at figure No. 290 A on page 76, is in 7 sizes for misses from 10 to 16 years old. For a miss of 12 years, it needs 2½ yards of cambric 36 inches wide, with 2¾ yards of embroidered edging 3¾ inches wide. Price of pattern, 10d. or 20 cents.

FIGURE NO. 290 A.— MISSES' HOUSE TOIL-
ETTE.—This consists of Misses' apron No. 4574 (copyright), shown on page 75; and costume No. 4565 (copyright), seen on page 44. Both patterns are in 7 sizes for misses from 10 to 16 years old: the apron costing 10d. or 20 cents; and the costume, 1s. 6d. or 35 cents. For goods needed, see pages 44 and 75.

FIGURE NO. 293 A.—MISSES' TOILETTE.
—This consists of Misses' Russian blouse No. 4612 (copyright), again shown on page 73; and bell skirt No. 4236 (copyright), seen on page 54. Both patterns are in 7 sizes for misses from 10 to 16 years of age: the blouse costing 1s. or 25 cents; and the skirt, 1s. 3d. or 30 cents. For a miss of 12 years, the blouse needs 4⅞ yards of goods 22 inches wide, or 2⅜ yards 44 inches wide. The skirt requires 3⅞ yards 22 inches wide, or 1⅞ yard 44 inches wide.

4572

No. 4572.—Ladies' Combing-Sack (Copyright).—At figure No. 279 A on page 78 this sack is again shown. It is here represented made of flannel and decorated with fancy stitching. The sleeve may be drawn in at the wrist by a shirr-tape or an elastic or allowed to flare in bell style, as preferred. The pattern is in 13 sizes for ladies from 28 to 46 inches, bust measure. For a lady of medium size, it requires $4\frac{1}{4}$ yards of goods 22 inches wide, or $3\frac{3}{4}$ yards 27 inches wide, or 3 yards 36 inches wide. If material 44 inches wide be chosen, $2\frac{1}{8}$ yards will suffice. Price of pattern, 1s. or 25 cents.

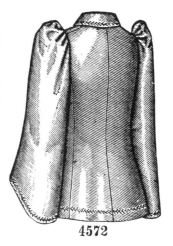

4572

4573

No. 4573.—Ladies' Single-Breasted Box Coat (Copyr't).—Another view of this stylish coat is given at figure No. 282 A on this page. It is here represented made of tan light-weight cloth and finished with a single row of stitching. The pattern is in 13 sizes for ladies from 28 to 46 inches, bust measure. For a lady of medium size, the garment will need $5\frac{1}{4}$ yards of material 22 inches wide, or $2\frac{7}{8}$ yards 44 inches wide. If goods 54 inches wide be used, $2\frac{1}{8}$ yards will be sufficient for the purpose. Price of pattern, 1s. 6d. or 35 cents.

4573

4602

No. 4602.—Misses' Russian Skirt (Copyright).—Other views of this stylish garment may be obtained by referring to figures Nos. 294 A and 289 A on pages 72 and 75. The skirt is here pictured developed in dress goods, prettily trimmed with Hercules and soutache braids. The pattern is in 7 sizes for misses from 10 to 16 years of age. To make the garment for a miss of 12 years, calls for 4 yards of goods 22 inches wide, or $3\frac{3}{8}$ yards 30 inches wide, or $2\frac{1}{8}$ yards 44 inches wide, or 2 yards 50 inches wide. Price of pattern, 1s. 3d. or 30 cts.

4602

Figure No. 262 A.—Ladies' Russian Toilette.—This consists of Ladies' Russian basque No. 4610 (copyr't), shown again on page 72; and Watteau skirt No. 4564 (copyr't), differently represented on page 34. The skirt pattern is in 9 sizes for ladies from 20 to 36 inches, waist measure, and costs 1s. 6d. or 35 cents. The basque pattern is in 13 sizes for ladies from 28 to 46 inches, bust measure, and costs 1s. 3d. or 30 cents. To make the toilette for a lady of medium size, calls for $11\frac{7}{8}$ yards of material 22 inches wide.

4583

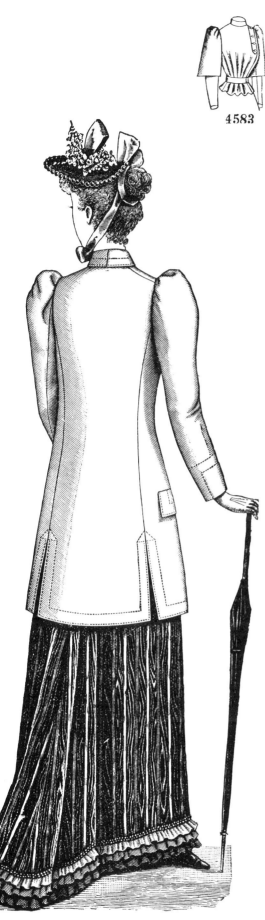

4583

4583

NO. 4583.—MISSES' RUSSIAN WAIST (WITH FITTED BODY-LINING) (Copyright).—At figure No. 294 A on page 72 of the present issue a different view of this waist is given. The pattern is in 7 sizes for misses from 10 to 16 years of age. To make the waist for a miss of 12 years, will require $3\frac{3}{8}$ yards of material 22 inches wide, or $2\frac{3}{4}$ yards 30 inches wide, or $1\frac{7}{8}$ yard 44 inches wide, or $1\frac{3}{4}$ yard 50 inches wide. Price of pattern, 10d. or 20 cents.

FIGURE NO. 299 A.—CHILD'S OUTDOOR TOILETTE.— This consists of Child's costume No. 4601 (copyright), shown on page 77; and hat No. 4593 (copyright), on page 78. The costume pattern is in 6 sizes for children from 2 to 7 years old, and costs 10d. or 20 cents. The hat pattern is in 4 sizes from 1 to 7 years old, and costs 5d. or 10 cents. Of goods 22 inches wide for a child of 5 years, the costume needs $3\frac{7}{8}$ yards, and the hat $1\frac{7}{8}$ yard.

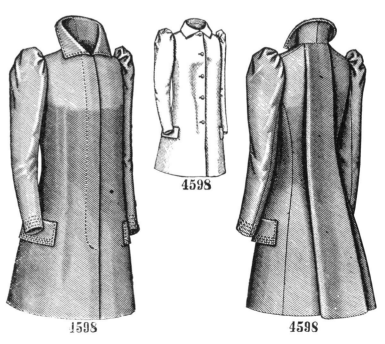

4598

4598

4598

FIGURE NO. 282 A.—LADIES' PROMENADE TOILETTE.— This consists of Ladies' coat No. 4573 (copyright), again represented on this page; and skirt No. 4582 (copyright), pictured on page 73. The coat pattern is in 13 sizes for ladies from 28 to 46 inches, bust measure, and costs 1s. 6d. or 35 cents. The skirt pattern is in 9 sizes for ladies from 20 to 36 inches, waist measure, and costs 1s. 6d. or 35 cents. Of one material for a lady of medium size, the toilette needs $11\frac{5}{8}$ yards 22 inches wide: the coat requiring $5\frac{1}{4}$ yards; and the skirt, $6\frac{3}{8}$ yards.

NO. 4598.—LADIES' COAT, WITH WATTEAU BACK (Copyright).—Other illustrations of this stylish coat may be observed by referring to figures Nos. 260 A and 261 A on page 78. Cloth was here chosen for the coat, and machine-stitching forms the completion. Tan. brown, dark-blue, mode or black melton, Bedford cord, faced cloth or coating will make up fashionably in this way, and a simple finish will generally be observed. The pattern is in 13 sizes for ladies from 28 to 46 inches, bust measure. For a lady of medium size, it requires $2\frac{3}{8}$ yards of goods 50 inches wide, or $2\frac{1}{4}$ yards 54 inches wide. Price of pattern, 1s. 6d. or 35 cents.

4613

4613

4613

NO. 4613.—LADIES' RUSSIAN COSTUME, WITH SLIGHT TRAIN (PERFORATED FOR ROUND LENGTH) (Copyright).—This costume is again portrayed at figure No. 268 A on page 75. Dress goods and velvet are here associated, and fancy silk gimp furnishes the ornamentation. The pattern is in 13 sizes for ladies from 28 to 46 inches, bust measure. In the combination shown for a lady of medium size, it requires $6\frac{1}{2}$ yards of dress goods 40 inches wide, and 3 yards of velvet. Of one material, it needs 13 yards 22 inches wide, or $6\frac{5}{8}$ yards 44 inches wide, or $6\frac{3}{8}$ yards 50 ins. wide. Price of pattern, 1s. 8d. or 40 cents.

4580

4580

NO. 4580.—GIRLS' RUSSIAN DRESS (Copyright).—Another view of this charming little dress is given at figure No. 297 A on page 72, where it is made of dark-blue serge and trimmed with Russian bands. Pink gingham is here represented in the dress, and narrow white braid decorates it prettily. The pattern is in 11 sizes for girls from 2 to 12 years of age. To make the garment for a girl of 8 years, needs $5\frac{1}{8}$ yards of material 22 inches wide, or 4 yards 30 inches wide, or $2\frac{5}{8}$ yards 44 inches wide. Price of pattern, 10d. or 20 cents.

FIGURE NO. 271 A.— LADIES' YOKE WRAPPER. —This depicts Ladies' yoke wrapper No. 4606 (copyr't), shown on page 74. The pattern is in 13 sizes for ladies from 28 to 46 inches, bust measure, and costs 1s. 6d. or 35 cents. For a lady of medium size, it requires $10\frac{3}{8}$ yards of material 22 inches wide.

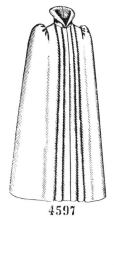

No. 4597.—LADIES' CAPE, WITH ATTACHED WATTEAU PLAIT (TO BE MADE WITH OR WITHOUT THE SHORT CAPE) (Copyright).—At figure No. 281 A on page 76 of this publication this cape may be seen differently developed. Tan cloth and écru *point de Gène* lace are united in the garment in the present instance. Capes of this kind will make up well in Bedford cord, faced cloth and similar materials, and the lace may be of any preferred variety in vogue. The pattern is in 10 sizes for ladies from 28 to 46 inches, bust measure. In the combination shown for a lady of medium size. it needs 4 yards of cloth 54 inches wide, and 2¼ yards of lace flouncing 19 inches wide. Of one material, it calls for 5 yards either 44, 50 or 54 inches wide. Price of pattern, 1s. 6d. or 35 cents.

4597

4597

4597

4592

4592

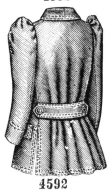

4592

FIGURE NO. 274 A.—LADIES' PROMENADE TOILETTE.— This consists of Ladies' tunic No. 4590 (copyright), which is again shown on page 75 of this publication; and costume No. 4571 (copyright), on page 16. For the sizes and prices of the patterns, and the quantities of materials required. refer to the pages just mentioned.

No. 4592.—GIRLS' BELTED JACKET (Copyright).—This jacket is pictured made of other materials at figure No. 296 A on page 72. It is here shown made of plain cloth and finished with machine-stitching. The fronts may be closed to the throat, or reversed to form lapels. The pattern is in 7 sizes for girls from 3 to 9 years old. For a girl of 8 years. it needs 3⅝ yards of goods 22 inches wide, or 1¾ yard 44 inches wide, or 1⅜ yard 54 inches wide. Price of pattern, 10d. or 20 cents.

FIGURE NO. 285 A.—MISSES' RUSSIAN TOILETTE.—This consists of Misses' Russian blouse No. 4607 (copyr't), shown on page 75; and bell skirt No. 4576 (copyr't), on page 75. The blouse pattern is in 7 sizes for misses from 10 to 16 years old, and costs 1s. or 25 cents. The skirt pattern is in 7 sizes for misses from 10 to 16 years old, and costs 1s. 3d. or 30 cts. Of one material for a miss of 12 years, the toilette requires 8⅝ yards 22 inches wide; the blouse calling for 4½ yards, and the skirt for 4⅛ yards

21

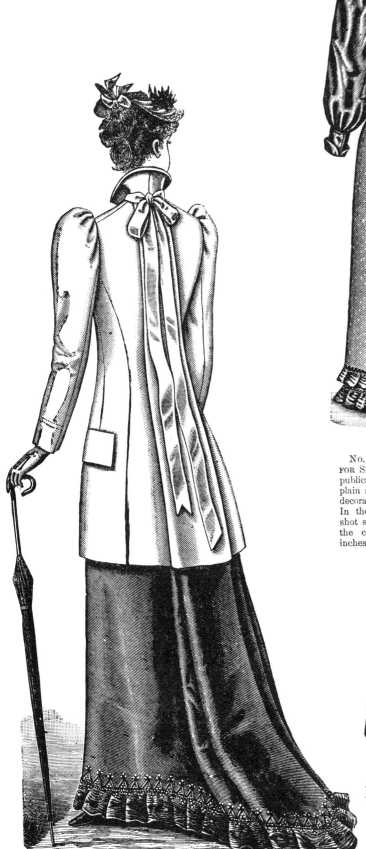

4614

4614

No. 4614.—Ladies' Corselet Princess Costume, with Demi-Train (Perforated for Slight Train) (Copyright).—By referring to figure No. 270 A on page 72 of this publication, another view of this stylish costume may be observed. Shot suiting and plain silk are here effectively united, and moiré ribbon and gimp provide handsome decoration. The pattern is in 13 sizes for ladies from 28 to 46 inches, bust measure. In the combination pictured for a lady of medium size, it will require $4\frac{3}{8}$ yards of shot suiting 40 inches wide, and $4\frac{1}{2}$ yards of plain silk 20 inches wide. To make the costume of one material, needs $10\frac{7}{8}$ yards 22 inches wide, or $5\frac{5}{8}$ yards 44 inches wide, or 5 yards 50 inches wide. Price of pattern, 1s. 8d. or 40 cents.

4581

4581

No. 4581.—Misses' Side-Plaited Blouse (With Fitted Linings) (Copyr't).—At figure No. 288 A on page 75 of this issue another view of this blouse may be observed. The pattern is in 9 sizes for misses from 8 to 16 years of age. Surah, India or China silk, faille or any pliable woollen or cotton fabric will make up nicely by the mode, with lace, embroidery, fancy stitching, etc., for decoration. To make the blouse for a miss of 12 years, will require $4\frac{1}{4}$ yards of material 22 inches wide, or $3\frac{3}{8}$ yards 30 inches wide, or $2\frac{1}{8}$ yards 44 or 50 inches wide. Price of pattern, 1s. or 25 cents.

Figure No. 260 A.—Ladies' Street Toilette.—This consists of Ladies' coat No. 4598 (copyright), shown on page 77; and skirt No. 4564 (copyright), on page 34. The coat pattern is in 13 sizes for ladies from 28 to 46 inches, bust measure, and costs 1s. 6d. or 35 cents. The skirt pattern is in 9 sizes for ladies from 20 to 36 inches, waist measure, and costs 1s. 6d. or 35 cents. For a lady of medium size, they require $5\frac{3}{4}$ yards of goods 50 inches wide: the coat needing $2\frac{3}{8}$ yards; and skirt, $3\frac{3}{8}$ yards.

4604

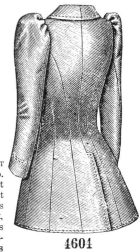

4604

4601

No. 4604.—MISSES' COAT (Copyright).—At figure No. 286 A on this page this coat is shown made up in different material. Dark cloth was here used for the garment, and machine-stitching forms a tasteful finish. The pattern is in 7 sizes for misses from 10 to 16 years of age. For a miss of 12 years, the garment requires 4¼ yards of goods 22 inches wide, or 2⅛ yards 44 inches wide. If material 54 inches wide be selected, then 1¾ yard will prove sufficient. Price of pattern, 1s. or 25 cents.

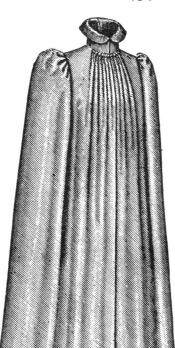

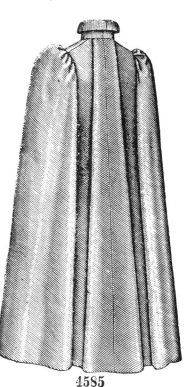

4585

4585

No. 4585.—LADIES' WATTEAU CAPE (Copyright). —Another view of this stylish cape is portrayed at figure No. 273 A on page 75 of this publication. In the present instance it is shown developed in light-weight cloth, and a perfectly plain finish is adopted. The pattern is in 10 sizes for ladies from 28 to 46 inches, bust measure. For a lady of medium size, the garment will need 5⅜ yards of material 22 inches wide, or 3¼ yards 44 inches wide, or 2¼ yards 54 inches wide. Price of pattern, 1s. 6d. or 35 cents.

4585

FIGURE NO. 266 A.—LADIES' TOILETTE.—This consists of Ladies' tunic No. 4591 (copyright), which is also seen on page 74 of this publication; basque No. 4570 (copyright), pictured on page 32; and skirt No. 4373 (copyright), also shown on page 35. A back view of the toilette is presented at figure No. 267 A on page 75. The tunic pattern is in 7 sizes for ladies from 28 to 40 inches, bust measure, and costs 1s. 3d. or 30 cents. The basque pattern is in 13 sizes for ladies from 28 to 46 inches, bust measure, and costs 1s. 3d. or 30 cents. The skirt pattern is in 9 sizes for ladies from 20 to 36 inches, waist measure, and costs 1s. 6d. or 35 cents. To make the toilette of one material for a lady of medium size, will require 15½ yards 22 inches wide.

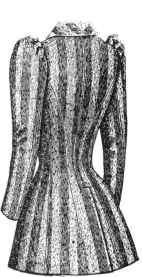

No. 4611.—LADIES' DRESSING-SACK (Copyright).—At figure No. 277 A on page 74 this sack may be again seen. It is here pictured made of striped flannel and plainly finished. Eiderdown flannel, cashmere, Henrietta cloth, French flannel and, in fact, all varieties of soft, pliable materials are adaptable to the mode, and any simple finish may be adopted. The pattern is in 13 sizes for ladies from 28 to 46 inches, bust measure. For a lady of medium size, the garment needs 4 yards of material 22 inches wide, or 3 yards 30 inches wide, or 2 yards 44 inches wide. Price of pattern, 1s. or 25 cents.

4611

4611

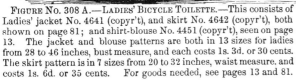

FIGURE NO. 308 A.—LADIES' BICYCLE TOILETTE.—This consists of Ladies' jacket No. 4641 (copyr't), and skirt No. 4642 (copyr't), both shown on page 81; and shirt-blouse No. 4451 (copyr't), seen on page 13. The jacket and blouse patterns are both in 13 sizes for ladies from 28 to 46 inches, bust measure, and each costs 1s. 3d. or 30 cents. The skirt pattern is in 7 sizes from 20 to 32 inches, waist measure, and costs 1s. 6d. or 35 cents. For goods needed, see pages 13 and 81.

FIGURE NO. 309 A.—LADIES' BICYCLE TOILETTE.— This consists of Ladies' skirt No. 4642 (copyright), which is again shown on page 81 of this publi-cation; blouse No. 4451 (copyright), also seen on page 13; and cap No. 3637 (copyright), pictured on page 14. For the sizes, prices and quantities of materials required, see pages 13, 14 and 81.

FIGURE NO. 336 A. — CHILD'S DRESS.—This illustrates Child's dress No. 4644 (copyright), differ-ently pictured on page 83 of this publication. The pattern is in 7 sizes for children from $\frac{1}{2}$ to 6 years of age, and costs 10d. or 20 cents. To make the dress in the combina-tion shown on page 83 for a child of 5 years, will require $2\frac{1}{2}$ yards of nainsook 36 inches wide, and $\frac{1}{4}$ yard of fancy tucking 27 inches wide. Of one material, it calls for $3\frac{1}{2}$ yards 22 inches wide, or $2\frac{1}{8}$ yards 36 inches wide, or $1\frac{3}{4}$ yard 44 inches wide.

4593

No. 4593.—LITTLE GIRLS' HAT (Copyright).—By referring to figure No. 299 A on page 76 of this publication, this useful little hat may be again seen. It is here represented made of chambray and trimmed with cordings of the material. Nainsook, cambric, plain, striped or checked gingham, percale, lawn, mull and all similar fabrics are suitable for hats of this kind, and the finish will usually be as illustrated in the accompanying engraving. The pattern is in 4 sizes for little girls from 1 to 7 years of age. To make the hat for a girl of 5 years, will need 1⅞ yard of material 22 inches wide, or 1⅝ yard 27 inches wide, or 1½ yard either 36 or 44 inches wide. Price of pattern, 5d. or 10 cents.

4635   **4635**

No. 4635.—MISSES' RUSSIAN BLOUSE (IN SURPLICE STYLE) (Copyright).—This blouse is again shown at figure No. 326 A on page 80. The pattern is in 7 sizes for misses from 10 to 16 years of age. For a miss of 12 years. it requires 4½ yards of goods 22 inches wide, or 3⅝ yards 30 inches wide, or 2⅜ yards 44 inches wide, or 2⅛ yards 50 inches wide. Price of pattern, 1s. or 25 cents.

4632   **4632**

No. 4632.—MISSES' RUSSIAN BLOUSE (Copyright).— Another illustration of this blouse is given at figure No. 329 A on this page. The pattern is in 7 sizes for misses from 10 to 16 years of age. To make the blouse of one material for a miss of 12 years, will require 5¾ yards 22 inches wide, or 4⅛ yards 30 inches wide, or 3 yards 44 inches wide. Price of pattern, 1s. or 25 cents.

FIGURE No. 286 A. — MISSES' STREET TOILETTE. —This consists of Misses' coat No. 4604 (copyright), shown again on this page; and costume No. 4410 (copyright), on page 44. Both patterns are in 7 sizes for misses from 10 to 16 years of age: the coat costing 1s. or 25 cents; and the costume, 1s. 6d. or 35 cents. For a miss of 12 years, the toilette needs 12½ yards of goods, 22 inches wide: the coat needing 4¼ yds.; and the costume, 8¼ yds.

FIGURE NO. 261 A.—LADIES' COAT.—This illustrates Ladies' coat No. 4598 (copyright), seen again on page 77. A back view of the garment, showing it made of pearl cloth, is displayed at figure No. 260 A on this page. Brown cloth was used for the coat in the present instance, and machine - stitching forms the completion. A large variety of seasonable coatings are adaptable to the mode. The pattern is in 13 sizes for ladies from 28 to 46 inches, bust measure, and costs 1s. 6d. or 35 cents. To make the coat for a lady of medium size, will call for 3⅜ yards of material 50 inches wide, or 2¼ yards 54 inches wide.

25

No. 4627.— GIRLS' GUIMPE (Copyright).— This pattern is in 8 sizes for girls from 2 to 9 years of age. For a girl of 8 years, the guimpe needs 2¼ yards of silk 20 inches wide, with 1 yard of cambric 27 inches wide. Of one material, it requires 2¾ yards 22 inches wide, or 2¼ yards 27 inches wide, or 1⅜ yard 44 inches wide. Price of pattern, 5d. or 10 cents.

4627

4627

No. 4639.— MISSES' COR-SELET, WITH SUSPENDERS (Copyr't). — At figure No. 324 A on page 80 this corselet may be again seen. The pattern is in 9 sizes for misses from 8 to 16 years old. Of one material for a miss of 12 years, it needs 1 yard 22 inches wide, or ⅝ yard 44 inches wide, or ½ yard 50 inches wide. Price of pattern, 7d. or 15 cents.

4639

4639

4619

4619

No. 4619.—LITTLE GIRLS' DRESS (TO BE WORN WITH A GUIMPE) (Copyright).—This pattern, also shown at figure No. 335 A on this page, is in 7 sizes for girls from 2 to 8 years of age. For a girl of 5 years, it needs 3 yards of spotted cashmere 40 ins. wide, and ¼ yard of velvet, cut bias. Of one material, it needs 5⅝ yards 22 inches wide, or 4¼ yards 30 inches wide, or 3 yards 44 inches wide. Price of pattern, 10d. or 20 cents.

FIGURE NO. 332 A.—MISSES' PROMENADE TOIL-ETTE.—This consists of Misses' jacket No. 4640 (copyright), shown again on page 81; and blouse No. 4015 (copyright), on page 53. Both patterns are in 7 sizes for misses from 10 to 16 years old, and each costs 1s. or 25 cents. Of material 22 inches wide for a miss of 12 years, the jacket needs 4½ yards, while the blouse requires 3¼ yards.

4638

4638

No. 4638.—GIRLS' DRESS (TO BE WORN WITH A GUIMPE) (Copyright).—This pretty little frock is de-picted again at figure No. 327 A on page 81. It is here pictured developed in plaid gingham and trimmed with embroidered edging and ribbon bows. The pat-tern is in 8 sizes for girls from 5 to 12 years of age. For a girl of 8 years, the dress calls for 3¼ yards of goods 22 inches wide, or 2½ yards 27 inches wide, or 2¼ yards 36 inches wide, or 1⅝ yard 44 inches wide. Price of pattern, 1s. or 25 cents.

FIGURE NO. 329 A.—MISSES' RUSSIAN BLOUSE. —This portrays Misses' blouse No. 4632 (copy-right), again represented on this page. The pattern is in 7 sizes for misses from 10 to 16 years of age, and costs 1s. or 25 cents. For a miss of 12 years, the garment requires 5¾ yards of material 22 inches wide, or 4⅛ yards 30 inches wide, or 3 yards 44 inches wide.

NO. 4594.—GIRLS' DRESS (TO BE WORN WITH A GUIMPE)
(Copyr't).—This pattern, again shown at figure No. 295 A on
page 74, is in 8 sizes for girls from 5 to 12 years old. For a
girl of 8 years, the dress needs $4\frac{1}{4}$ yards of material 22 inches
wide, or $3\frac{5}{8}$ yards 27 inches wide, or $2\frac{5}{8}$ yards 36 inches wide,
or $2\frac{1}{4}$ yards 44 inches wide. Price of pattern, 1s. or 25 cents.

NO. 4628.—LADIES' WATTEAU COAT (Copyright).—At figure No.
303 A on page 82 this stylish coat is again shown. Cloth was here selected for the garment. Any seasonable variety of coating will develop
nicely by the mode. The pattern is in 13 sizes for ladies from 28 to 46
inches, bust measure. To make the coat for a lady of medium size, will
require $6\frac{3}{8}$ yards of material 22 inches wide, or $3\frac{3}{8}$ yards 44 inches
wide, or $2\frac{3}{4}$ yards 54 inches wide. Price of pattern, 1s. 6d. or 35 cents.

FIGURE NO. 335 A.—LITTLE GIRLS'
TOILETTE.—This consists of Little
Girls' dress No. 4619 (copyr't), shown
again on this page; and guimpe No.
4013 (copyright), on page 61. The
dress pattern is in 7 sizes for little girls
from 2 to 8 years of age, and costs 10d.
or 20 cents. The guimpe pattern is in
6 sizes for little girls from 2 to 7 years
of age, and costs 5d. or 10 cents. For
a girl of 5 years, the dress requires
$5\frac{5}{8}$ yards of material 22 inches wide,
or 3 yards 44 inches wide. The
guimpe needs $1\frac{3}{4}$ yard 22 inches
wide, or $\frac{7}{8}$ yard 44 inches wide.

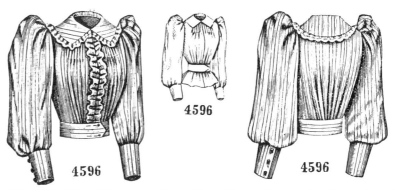

NO. 4596.—MISSES' BLOUSE OR SHIRT-WAIST (Copyright).—Another illustration of
this dainty waist is portrayed at figure No. 291 A on page 73. Striped wash silk
was here chosen for making the blouse, and ruffles of the material and buttons provide
the decoration. The mode will develop charmingly in all sorts of washable materials, and lace, ruffles of the material or any simple garniture may be applied. The
pattern is in 9 sizes for misses from 8 to 16 years of age. For a miss of 12 years,
it needs 4 yards of goods 22 inches wide, or $3\frac{1}{2}$ yards 27 inches wide, or $2\frac{1}{2}$ yards
36 inches wide, or 2 yards 44 inches wide. Price of pattern, 1s. or 25 cents.

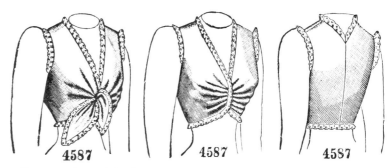

NO. 4587.—LADIES' BOLÉRO CORSET-COVER (Copyright).—The engravings picture
a corset-cover developed in nainsook, with embroidered edging for decoration.
The pattern is in 10 sizes for ladies from 28 to 46 inches, bust measure.
For a lady of medium size, the tied corset-cover will need $1\frac{1}{4}$ yard of goods 20
inches wide, or 1 yard 36 inches wide; while the other requires 1 yard 20
inches wide, or $\frac{7}{8}$ yard 36 inches wide. Price of pattern, 7d. or 15 cents.

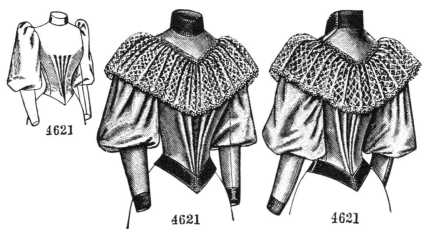

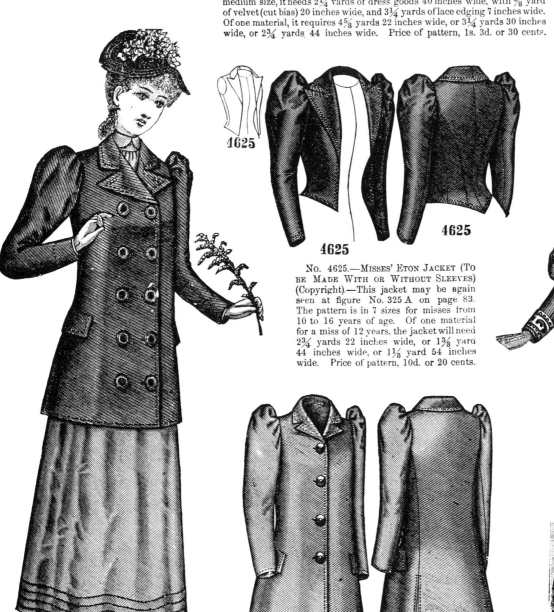

No. 4621.—LADIES' BASQUE (Copyright).—At figure No. 313 A on page 82 this basque is again shown. The pattern is in 13 sizes for ladies from 28 to 46 inches, bust measure. In the combination shown for a lady of medium size, it needs $2\frac{1}{4}$ yards of dress goods 40 inches wide, with $\frac{5}{8}$ yard of velvet (cut bias) 20 inches wide, and $3\frac{1}{4}$ yards of lace edging 7 inches wide. Of one material, it requires $4\frac{5}{8}$ yards 22 inches wide, or $3\frac{1}{4}$ yards 30 inches wide, or $2\frac{3}{4}$ yards 44 inches wide. Price of pattern, 1s. 3d. or 30 cents.

No. 4625.—MISSES' ETON JACKET (TO BE MADE WITH OR WITHOUT SLEEVES) (Copyright).—This jacket may be again seen at figure No. 325 A on page 83. The pattern is in 7 sizes for misses from 10 to 16 years of age. Of one material for a miss of 12 years. the jacket will need $2\frac{3}{4}$ yards 22 inches wide, or $1\frac{3}{8}$ yard 44 inches wide, or $1\frac{1}{8}$ yard 54 inches wide. Price of pattern, 10d. or 20 cents.

FIGURE NO. 330 A.—MISSES' TOILETTE. This consists of Misses' belted coat No. 4633 (copyright), which is also seen on page 81; and costume No. 4649 (copyright), shown again on this page. Both patterns are in 7 sizes for misses from 10 to 16 years old : the coat costing 1s. 3d. or 30 cts. ; and the costume, 1s. 6d. or 35 cts. For goods needed, see pages 80 and 81.

No. 4629.—MISSES' SACK OR BOX COAT (Copyright). — This coat, shown again at figure No. 331 A on page 83, is here represented made of mode cloth. The pattern is in 9 sizes for misses from 8 to 16 years of age. To make the coat for a miss of 12 years, will require $4\frac{1}{8}$ yards of material 22 inches wide, or $1\frac{7}{8}$ yard 44 inches wide. If goods 54 inches wide be used, $1\frac{5}{8}$ yard will suffice. Price of pattern, 1s. 3d or 30 cents.

FIGURE NO. 326A.—MISSES' TOILETTE. —This consists of Misses' Russian blouse No. 4635 (copyright), also shown on page 79; and bell skirt No. 4576 (copyright), seen on page 75. For sizes, prices, and goods needed see pages 75 and 79.

4630   4630

No. 4630.—Ladies' Russian Jacket, with Watteau Back (Copyright).—Another view of this jacket is given at figure No. 306 A on page 82. Cloth was here used in the development, and feather trimming supplies the decoration. Top garments of this kind are very popular for wear on cool days in Summer, and they may be made up individually or *en suite*. The pattern is in 13 sizes for ladies from 28 to 46 inches, bust measure. For a lady of medium size, the jacket requires 5⅞ yards of material 22 inches wide, or 2⅞ yards 44 inches wide, or 2⅜ yards 54 inches wide. Price of pattern, 1s. 6d. or 35 cts.

4649   4649

Figure No. 311 A.—Ladies' Toilette.—This consists of Ladies' skirt No. 4631 (copyright), also shown on page 83 of this publication; jacket No. 4645 (copyright), seen again on this page; and basque No. 4348 (copyright), pictured on page 37. The jacket pattern is in 13 sizes for ladies from 28 to 46 inches, bust measure, and costs 10d. or 20 cents. The basque pattern is in 14 sizes for ladies from 28 to 48 inches, bust measure, and costs 1s. 3d. or 30 cents. The skirt pattern is in 9 sizes for ladies from 20 to 36 inches. waist measure, and costs 1s. 6d. or 35 cents. For a lady of medium size, they need 12¾ yards of goods 22 inches wide.

No. 4649.—Misses' Costume, with Bell Skirt (Copyright).—At figures Nos. 328 A, 330 A and 331 A on pages 80 and 83 this costume is again shown. The pattern is in 7 sizes for misses from 10 to 16 years of age. For a miss of 12 years, it calls for 2⅞ yards of dress goods 40 inches wide, with 2⅞ yards of Bengaline 20 inches wide. Of one material, it needs 6¾ yards 22 inches wide, or 5⅜ yards 30 inches wide, or 3⅜ yards 44 inches wide. Price of pattern, 1s. 6d. or 35 cents.

4620

4620

4620

No. 4620.—LADIES' CAPE, WITH WATTEAU BACK (Copyright).—This pattern, shown again at figure No. 302 A on page 82, is in 10 sizes for ladies from 28 to 46 inches, bust measure. For a lady of medium size, the cape will call for 6¼ yards of material 22 inches wide, or 3 yards 44 inches wide, or 2½ yards 54 inches wide. Price of pattern, 1s. 6d. or 35 cents.

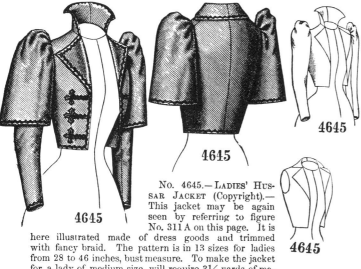

4645

4645

4645

4645

4645

No. 4645.—LADIES' HUSSAR JACKET (Copyright).—This jacket may be again seen by referring to figure No. 311 A on this page. It is here illustrated made of dress goods and trimmed with fancy braid. The pattern is in 13 sizes for ladies from 28 to 46 inches, bust measure. To make the jacket for a lady of medium size, will require 3½ yards of material 22 inches wide, or 1¾ yard 44 inches wide, or 1⅝ yard 50 inches wide. Price of pattern, 10d. or 20 cents.

No. 4601.—CHILD'S COSTUME (CLOSED IN RUSSIAN FASHION) (Copyright).—This pattern, again shown at figure No. 299 A on page 76, is in 6 sizes for children from 2 to 7 years old. For a child of 5 years, the costume needs 3⅞ yards of goods 22 inches wide, or 3¼ yards 30 inches wide, or 2¼ yards 44 inches wide. Price of pattern, 10d. or 20 cts.

4601

4601

FIGURE NO. 314 A.—LADIES' COSTUME.—This illustrates Ladies' costume No. 4647 (copyright), also seen on page 82. The pattern is in 13 sizes for ladies from 28 to 46 inches, bust measure, and costs 1s. 8d. or 40 cents. Of one material for a lady of medium size, it requires 9 yards 22 inches wide.

No. 4622. — LADIES'
DRESS SLEEVE (Copyright).
—A plain variety of dress
goods was selected for
making the pretty dress
sleeve here pictured. The
coat sleeve may be cut
away below the puff, and a
falling frill of lace may
trim the edge, if desired. The
pattern is in 7 sizes for ladies
from 9 to 15 inches, arm measure, measuring the arm about
an inch below the bottom of the
arm's-eye. To make a pair of
sleeves for a lady whose arm
measures 11 inches as described, needs 1⅞ yard of goods 22
inches wide, or 1¾ yard 30 inches wide, or 1⅛ yard 44 inches
wide, or 1 yard 50 inches wide.
Price of pattern, 5d. or 10 cents.

4622

4622

4622

FIGURE NO. 324 A.—MISSES' TOILETTE.
—This consists of Misses' corselet No.
4639 (copyright), which is again shown
on page 79; and guimpe No. 4579 (copyright), seen on page 75. The corselet
pattern is in 9 sizes for misses from 8
to 16 years old, and costs 7d. or 15
cents. The guimpe pattern is in 7 sizes
for misses from 10 to 16 years old, and
costs 7d. or 15 cents. Of goods 22 inches
wide for a miss of 12 years, the corselet
needs 1 yard, and the guimpe, 5¼ yards.

FIGURE NO. 322 A.—LADIES' *Négligé* TOILETTE.—This consists of Ladies' dressing-sack No. 4643 (copyright), shown
on page 83; and bell petticoat No. 4523 (copyright), on
page 39. The sack pattern is in 14 sizes for ladies from
28 to 48 inches, bust measure; the petticoat pattern is in
9 sizes for ladies from 20 to 36 inches, waist measure, and
each costs 1s. or 25 cents. For a lady of medium size, the
toilette needs 9⅜ yards of material 22 inches wide; the
sack requiring 4 yards, and the petticoat, 5⅜ yards.

FIGURE NO. 334 A.—MISSES' TOILETTE.—
This consists of Misses' hussar jacket No. 4646
(copyr't), seen on page 82; and blouse-waist
No. 4223 (copyr't), on page 52. Both patterns
are in 7 sizes for misses from 10 to 16 years
old: the jacket costing 7d. or 15 cts.; and the
blouse-waist, 1s. or 25 cts. Of goods 22 inches wide for a miss of 12 years, the jacket
needs 3 yards, and the blouse-waist, 3⅞ yards.

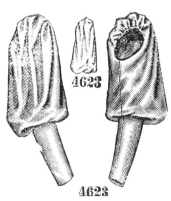

4623

4623

NO. 4623. — MISSES' AND GIRLS'
DRESS SLEEVE (Copyright).—This pattern is in 7 sizes from 4 to 16 years old.
For a miss of 12 years, a pair of sleeves
needs 1⅜ yard of material 22 inches
wide, or ⅞ yard 44 or 50 inches wide.
Price of pattern, 5d. or 10 cents.

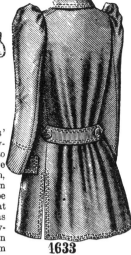

4633

4633

No. 4633.—Misses'
Belted Coat (Copy-
right).—By referring to
figure No. 330 A on page
80 of this publication,
this coat may be again
seen. The fronts may be
buttoned to the throat
or reversed in lapels, as
illustrated in the engravings. The pattern is in
7 sizes for misses from
10 to 16 years of age.

To make the garment for a miss of 12 years, will require 4¼ yards of material
22 inches wide, or 2 yards 44 inches wide. If goods 54 inches wide be selected,
then 1¾ yard will prove sufficient. Price of pattern, 1s. 3d. or 30 cents.

4640

4640

4640

No. 4640.—
Misses' Belted
Jacket or
Blazer (Copy-
right).—Another
portrayal of this
comfortable
jacket is depic-
ted at figure

No. 332 A on page 79. Cloth is the material here represented in the garment,
and machine-stitching forms a stylish completion. The pattern is in 7 sizes
for misses from 10 to 16 years of age. To make the garment for a miss
of 12 years, requires 4½ yards of goods 22 inches wide, or 2⅛ yards
44 inches wide, or 1¾ yard 54 inches wide. Price of pattern, 1s. or 25 cents.

FIGURE No. 317 A.—LADIES' TOILETTE.—This consists of Ladies'
Princess skirt No. 4650 (copyr't), again seen on this page; and blouse
No. 4349 (copyr't), on page 12. The skirt pattern is in 9 sizes for ladies
from 20 to 36 ins., waist meas., and costs 1s. 6d. or 35 cts. The blouse
pattern is in 13 sizes from 28 to 46 ins., bust meas., and costs 1s. 3d. or 30
cts. For a lady of medium size, they need 10⅝ yds. of goods 22 ins wide.

4651

4651

4651

No. 4651.—
Ladies' Belted
Jacket or
Blazer (Copy-
right).—At figure
No. 320 A on page
82 this stylish
jacket is again
portrayed. The
pattern is in 13
sizes for ladies

from 28 to 46 inches, bust measure. Cloth, cheviot, serge, flannel or any suitable
coating may be developed by the mode, and a plain finish will usually be adopted.
For a lady of medium size, it needs 5⅜ yards of goods 22 inches wide, or 2¾ yards
44 inches wide, or 2½ yards 54 inches wide. Price of pattern, 1s. 3d. or 30 cents.

4642

4642

4642

No. 4642.—Ladies' Bicycle Skirt (Copyright).—By referring to figures Nos. 308 A and 309 A on page 79, this skirt may be again seen. Navy-blue serge was here employed in making the skirt. The garment may be shortened to any desired length by lifting the skirt and drawing the ribbons through the rings sewed near the ends of the darts and to the seams. If the close effect at the back be desired, the lap may be buttoned. The pattern is in 7 sizes for ladies from 20 to 32 inches, waist measure. For a lady of medium size, it requires 4¾ yards of goods 30 inches wide, or 4¾ yards 44 inches wide, or 3½ yards 50 inches wide. Price of pattern, 1s. 6d. or 35 cents.

Figure No. 318 A.—Ladies' Toilette.—This consists of Ladies' Princess skirt No. 4650 (copyr't), shown again on this page; and waist No. 3877 (copyr't), on page 29. The skirt pattern is in 9 sizes for ladies from 20 to 36 inches, waist measure, and costs 1s. 6d. or 35 cents. The waist pattern is in 13 sizes for ladies from 28 to 46 inches, bust measure, and costs 1s. or 25 cents. Of material 44 inches wide for a lady of medium size, the skirt needs 3⅝ yards, and the waist, 1½ yard.

4650

4650

4650

4650

4650

No. 4650.—Ladies' Princess Skirt, with Suspenders and Slight Train (Perforated for Round Length) (Copyright).—This skirt is again illustrated at figures Nos. 317 A and 318 A on this page. The pattern is in 9 sizes for ladies from 20 to 36 inches, waist measure. To make the skirt of one material for a lady of medium size, needs 6¾ yards 22 inches wide, or 4⅛ yards 30 inches wide, or 3⅝ yards 44 inches wide, or 2⅝ yards 50 inches wide. Price of pattern, 1s. 6d. or 35 cts.

FIGURE NO. 303 A.—LADIES' WAT-
TEAU COAT.—This illustrates Ladies'
Watteau coat No. 4628 (copyright),
which is again pictured on page 79.
The pattern is in 13 sizes for ladies
from 28 to 46 inches, bust measure,
and costs 1s. 6d. or 35 cents. To make
the coat of one material for a lady of
medium size, will require 6⅜ yards
22 inches wide, or 3⅜ yards 44 inches
wide, or 2¾ yards 54 inches wide.

1634

4634   **4634**

1634

NO. 4634.—LADIES' ETON JACKET
(TO BE MADE WITH OR WITHOUT
SLEEVES) (Copyright).—By referring
to figure No. 312 A on this page,
this jacket may be again seen. Lin-
coln-green cloth is here pictured
in the jacket, and machine-stitching
finishes all the loose edges. The
pattern is in 13 sizes for ladies from
28 to 46 inches, bust measure. To
make the jacket for a lady of medium size, will require 3⅛ yards of
material 22 inches wide, or 1⅝ yard
44 inches wide, or 1⅜ yard 54 inches
wide. Price of pattern, 1s. or 25 cts.

NO. 4624.—CHILD'S
CREEPING APRON
(Copyr't).—This pro-
tective little apron is
shown made of check-
ed gingham and deco-
rated at the neck and
wrists with frills of
the material. All
sorts of washable ma-
terials may be used
for making the gar-
ment, and frills of em-
broidery or of the ma-
terial will generally
trim it. The pattern
is in one size,
and needs 2¼ yards of material 27
inches wide, or 1¾ yard 36 inches
wide. Price of pattern, 7d. or 15 cents.

4624   **4624**

FIGURE NO. 312 A.—LADIES' PROMENADE TOIL-
ETTE.—This consists of Ladies' Eton jacket No.
4634 (copyright), which is shown again on this
page; skirt No. 4631 (copyright), also pictured
on page 83; and vest No. 3384 (copyright), seen
again on page 19 of this issue. For the sizes and
prices of the patterns and the quantities of materials required, refer to the above-mentioned pages.

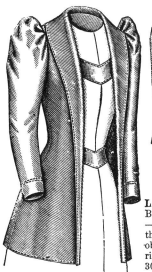

4641

NO. 4641.—
LADIES' JACKET OR
BLAZER (Copyr't).
—Another view of
this jacket may be
observed by refer-
ring to figure No.
308 A on page 79
of this publication.
It is here pictured

4641   **4641**

developed in cloth and finished with machine-stitching. The pattern is in 13
sizes for ladies from 28 to 46 inches, bust measure. For a lady of medium
size, it will need 5⅜ yards of material 22 inches wide, or 2⅝ yards 44 inches
wide, or 2⅛ yards 54 inches wide. Price of pattern, 1s. 3d. or 30 cents.

4616

4646

4646

4646

No. 4646.—MISSES' HUSSAR JACKET (Copyright).—This jacket is again displayed at figure No. 334 A on page 80. The pattern is in 7 sizes for misses from 10 to 16 years of age. To make the jacket for a miss of 12 years, requires 3 yards of goods 22 inches wide, or 1½ yard 44 inches wide, or 1¼ yard 54 inches wide. Price of pattern, 7d. or 15 cents.

4648

4648

4648

4648

No. 4648. — LADIES' WRAPPER, WITH DEMI-TRAIN (PERFORATED FOR ROUND LENGTH) (DESIRABLE FOR STOUT LADIES) (Copyright).—This wrapper may be seen differently made up by referring to figures Nos. 321 A and 323 A on page 83 of this publication. Striped dress goods were used for making the wrapper in the present instance, and a perfectly plain finish was observed. Pretty wrappers may be made of gingham, dimity, cashmere or any preferred dress fabric, and garniture may be added as fancy may suggest. The pattern is in 13 sizes for ladies from 30 to 48 inches, bust measure. To make the wrapper for a lady of medium size, requires 10¼ yards of material 22 inches wide, or 7⅜ yards 30 inches wide, or 5½ yards 44 inches wide, or 5¼ yards 50 inches wide. Price of pattern, 1s. 6d. or 35 cents.

FIGURE NO. 313 A.—LADIES' CARRIAGE TOILETTE.—This consists of Ladies' basque No. 4621 (copyright), shown again on page 79; and skirt No. 4631 (copyright), also seen on page 83. The basque pattern is in 13 sizes for ladies from 28 to 46 inches, bust measure, and costs 1s. 3d. or 30 cents. The skirt pattern is in 9 sizes for ladies from 20 to 36 inches, waist measure, and costs 1s. 6d. or 35 cents. For a lady of medium size, the toilette will require 10⅝ yards of material 22 inches wide.

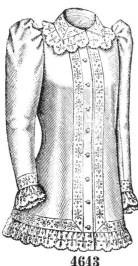

4643

No. 4643.— LADIES' DRESS-ING-SACK (Copyright). — This sack is also shown at figure No. 322 A on page 81. In the present instance it is pictured made of sheer white cambric, prettily trimmed with Hamburg insertion and edging. Sacks of this description will develop charmingly in lawn, wash silk, flannel or any other suitable material, and lace, tucks, ruffles or bias bands of the material, or any dainty but simple garniture may be added. The pattern is in 14 sizes for ladies from 28 to 48 inches, bust measure. To make the garment for a lady of medium size, will require 4 yards of material 22 inches wide, or $3\frac{1}{4}$ yards 27 inches wide, or $2\frac{5}{8}$ yards 36 inches wide, or 2 yards 44 inches wide. Price of pattern, 1s. or 25 cents.

4643

FIGURE No. 302 A. — LADIES' CAPE.—This illustrates Ladies' cape No. 4620 (copyright), which is shown differently developed on page 80 of this publication. Light-weight cloth is the material pictured in this instance, with velvet and *cabochon* trimming for decoration. The pattern is in 10 sizes for ladies from 28 to 46 inches, bust measure, and costs 1s. 6d. or 35 cents. To make the cape for a lady of medium size, needs $6\frac{1}{4}$ yards of material 22 inches wide, or 3 yards 44 inches wide, or $2\frac{1}{2}$ yards 54 inches wide.

4647

4647

4644

No. 4647.— LADIES' COSTUME, WITH SLIGHT TRAIN (PERFORATED FOR ROUND LENGTH) (Copyright).— Light cheviot is represented in this costume at figure No. 314 A on page 80, velvet, jet passementerie and silk spiral ruching forming the garniture. A charming Summer costume is here pictured developed in Nile-green crépon, the ornamentation consisting of lace net and edging, velvet ribbon and jet gimp. The pattern is in 13 sizes for ladies from 28 to 46 inches, bust measure. To make the costume for a lady of medium size, will require 9 yards of material 22 inches wide, or $6\frac{3}{4}$ yards 30 inches wide, or $4\frac{5}{8}$ yards 44 inches wide, or $4\frac{3}{8}$ yards 50 inches wide. Price of pattern, 1s. 8d. or 40 cents.

No. 4644.—CHILD'S DRESS (Copyright).— This pattern, shown again at figure No. 336 A on page 79, is in 7 sizes for children from $\frac{1}{2}$ to 6 years old. In the combination shown for a child of 5 years, it requires $2\frac{1}{2}$ yards of nainsook 36 inches wide, with $\frac{1}{4}$ yard of fancy tucking 27 inches wide. Of one material, the dress needs $3\frac{1}{2}$ yards 22 inches wide, or $2\frac{1}{3}$ yards 36 inches wide, or $1\frac{3}{4}$ yard 44 inches wide. Price of pattern, 10d. or 20 cents.

4644

FIGURE NO. 306 A.—LADIES' RUSSIAN JACKET.—
This illustrates Ladies' Russian jacket No. 4630 (copyright), shown on page 80. The pattern is in 13 sizes for ladies from 28 to 46 inches, bust measure, and costs 1s. 6d. or 35 cents. For a lady of medium size, it requires 5⅞ yards of goods 22 inches wide.

FIGURE NO. 327 A.—GIRLS' TOILETTE.—
This consists of Girls' dress No. 4638 (copyright), on page 79; and guimpe No. 4478 (copyright), on page 52. The dress pattern is in 8 sizes for girls from 5 to 12 years old, and costs 1s. or 25 cents. The guimpe pattern is in 11 sizes from 2 to 12 years old, and costs 5d. or 10 cents. Of goods 22 inches wide for a girl of 8 years, the guimpe needs 4 yards, and the dress, 3¼ yards.

FIGURE NO. 320 A.—LADIES' OUTING TOILETTE.—
This consists of Ladies' jacket No. 4651 (copyright), shown on page 81; and vest No. 4145 (copyright), seen on page 19. The jacket pattern is in 13 sizes for ladies from 28 to 46 inches, bust measure, and costs 1s. 3d. or 30 cents. The vest pattern is in 3 sizes— small, medium and large, and costs 5d. or 10 cents. For the materials needed, see pages 19 and 81.

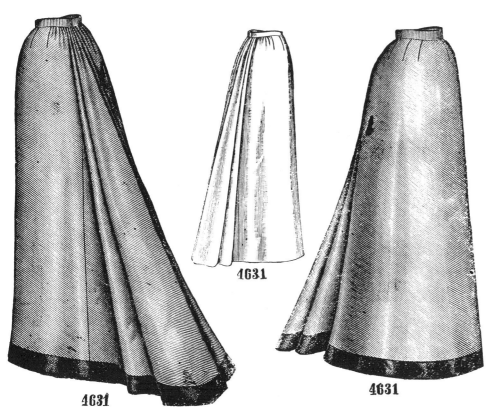

4631

4631

4631

NO. 4631.—LADIES' SKIRT, WITH A SLIGHT TRAIN (PERFORATED FOR ROUND LENGTH) (KNOWN AS THE CORNET SKIRT) (Copyright).—This skirt, which is one of the season's latest novelties, is also shown at figures Nos. 311 A, 312 A and 313 A on pages 80 and 82. The pattern is in 9 sizes for ladies from 20 to 36 inches, waist measure. To make the garment for a lady of medium size, will require 6 yards of goods 22 inches wide, or 4¾ yards 30 inches wide, or 2⅞ yards 44 inches wide, or 2⅝ yards 50 inches wide. Price of pattern, 1s. 6d. or 35 cents.

No. 4618.—Men's Night-Shirt, without a Collar.—Cambric, muslin and cotton cheviot are liked for men's night-shirts. This pattern is in 10 sizes for men from 32 to 50 inches, breast measure. For a man of medium size, it requires 5½ yards of goods 27 inches wide, or 4¾ yards 36 inches wide. Price of pattern, 1s. or 25 cents.

4637   **4637**

Figure No. 323 A.—Ladies' Wrapper.—This illustrates Ladies' wrapper No. 4618 (copyright), three views of which may be obtained by referring to page 82 of this publication. In the present instance the garment is pictured developed in figured challis and changeable silk. The pattern is in 13 sizes for ladies from 30 to 48 inches, bust measure, and costs 1s. 6d. or 35 cents. To make the wrapper for a lady of medium size, will require 10¼ yards of goods 22 inches wide, or 7⅜ yards 30 inches wide, or 5½ yards 44 inches wide, or 5¼ yards 50 inches wide.

No. 4637.—Ladies' Long Apron, with Sailor Collar (Copyright).—By referring to figure No. 321 A on this page, another view of this serviceable apron may be obtained. Striped gingham is pictured in the apron in the present instance, and embroidered edging trims it daintily. The pattern is in 5 sizes for ladies from 30 to 46 inches, bust measure. To make the garment for a lady of medium size, will require 2⅝ yards of material 27 inches wide, or 2⅛ yards of goods 36 inches wide. Price of pattern, 10d. or 20 cents.

FIGURE NO. 321 A.—LADIES' WORKING TOIL-
ETTE.—This consists of Ladies' wrapper No. 4648
(copyright), also shown on page 82; and apron
No. 4637 (copyright), again pictured on this page.
The wrapper pattern is in 13 sizes for ladies from
30 to 48 ins., bust measure, and costs 1s. 6d. or 35
cents.   The apron pattern is in 5 sizes for ladies
from 30 to 46 inches, bust measure, and costs 10 d.
or 20 cents.   For a lady of medium size, the wrapper needs 10¼ yards of goods 22 inches wide,
while the apron requires 2⅝ yards 27 ins. wide.

4652   **4652**

NO. 4652.—LADIES' SACK NIGHT-GOWN, WITH YOKE FACING.—
This pattern is in 13 sizes for ladies from 28 to 46 inches, bust
measure.   To make the garment for a lady of medium size, will
require 7⅜ yards of material 22 inches wide, or 4⅞ yards of
goods 36 inches wide.   Price of pattern, 1s. 3d. or 30 cents.

FIGURE NO. 331 A.—MISSES' OUTDOOR TOIL-
ETTE.—This consists of Misses' box coat No.
4629 (copyright), and costume No. 4649 (copyright), both shown again on page 80.   For the
sizes, prices, and goods needed, refer to page 80.

39

No. 4626.—
Misses' Guimpe
(Copyright). —
Surah and cam-
bric are unit-
ed in the dainty
guimpe here pic-
tured, and fancy
stitching trims it.
The pattern is in
7 sizes for misses
from 10 to 16
years of age, and
will develop dain-
tily in mull, China
or India silk and
other soft tex-
tures. For a miss

4626   **4626**

of 12 years, it needs $3\frac{3}{4}$ yards of goods 22 inches wide, or $3\frac{1}{4}$ yards 27 inches wide, or $2\frac{1}{4}$ yards 36 inches wide, or $1\frac{3}{4}$ yard 44 inches wide. In the combination shown, it requires $2\frac{3}{4}$ yards of Surah 20 inches wide, and $1\frac{1}{8}$ yard of cambric 27 inches wide. Price of pattern, 7d. or 15 cents.

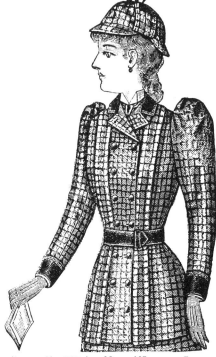

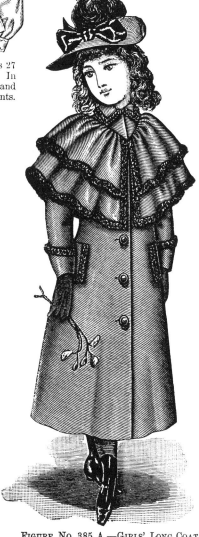

FIGURE NO. 384 A.—GIRLS' LONG COAT.—This is Girls' long coat No. 4662 (copyright), which is again portrayed on this page. The pattern is in 8 sizes for girls from 5 to 12 years old, and costs 1s. 3d. or 30 cents. For a girl of 8 years, it needs $5\frac{7}{8}$ yards of goods 22 inches wide, or $2\frac{7}{8}$ yards 44 inches wide, or $2\frac{1}{4}$ yards 54 inches wide.

FIGURE NO. 375 A.—MISSES' NORFOLK JACKET AND CAP.—This consists of Misses' long basque No. 4720 (copyright), shown on page 93; and cap No. 2175, on page 14. The basque pattern is in 7 sizes for misses from 10 to 16 years old, and costs 1s. or 25 cents. The cap pattern is in 7 sizes from 6 to $7\frac{1}{2}$, hat sizes, or from $19\frac{1}{4}$ to $23\frac{3}{4}$ inches, head measures, and costs 5d. or 10 cents. Of goods 22 ins. wide for a miss of 12 years, the basque needs $4\frac{1}{2}$ yards. A No. 7 cap needs $\frac{3}{4}$ yd. 22 ins. wide.

FIGURE NO. 385 A.—GIRLS' LONG COAT.— This portrays Girls' long coat No. 4687 (copy-right), again depicted on page 85. The pattern is in 10 sizes for girls from 3 to 12 years of age, and costs 1s. 3d. or 30 cents. To make the garment for a girl of 8 years, requires $6\frac{1}{2}$ yards of material 22 inches wide, or $3\frac{1}{4}$ yards 44 inches wide, or $2\frac{5}{8}$ yards 54 inches wide.

4715   **4715**

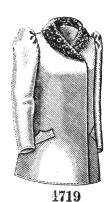

No. 4715. — LITTLE BOYS' BLOUSE COSTUME. —At figure No. 397 A on page 93 this costume may be again seen. The pattern is in 6 sizes for

4715

little boys from 2 to 7 years old. For a boy of 5 years, it needs $3\frac{3}{4}$ yards of striped and 1 yard of plain flannel 27 inches wide. Price, 1s. or 25 cts.

No. 4719.—
GIRLS' JACK-
ET(Copyright).
— Another
view of this
jacket may be
obtained at fig-
ure No. 386 A
on this page.
The pattern is

4719

in 8 sizes for girls from 5 to 12 years of age. For a girl of 8 years, the jacket re-quires $1\frac{1}{4}$ yard of cloth and $\frac{7}{8}$ yard of Astrakhan each 54 inches wide. Of one material, it needs $3\frac{1}{4}$ yards 22 inches wide, or

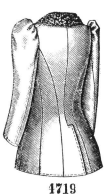

4719   **4719**

$1\frac{5}{8}$ yard 44 inches wide. If goods 54 inches wide be selected, then $1\frac{3}{8}$ yard will prove sufficient. Price of pattern, 10d. or 20 cents.

—This portrays Girls' jacket No. 4719 (copyright), shown again on this page. The pattern is in 8 sizes for girls from 5 to 12 years of age, and costs 10d. or 20 cents. To make the jacket for a girl of 8 years, will require 3¼ yards of goods 22 inches wide, or 1⅝ yard 44 inches wide, or 1⅜ yard 54 inches wide.

4662   **4662**

No. 4662.—GIRLS' LONG COAT (Copyright).— This coat is again portrayed at figure No. 384 A on this page. It is here pictured developed in cloth, with fur for trimming. Melton, cloth, kersey and Bedford cord are especially well adapted to the mode, and braid or machine-stitching may form the trimming. A plain finish, however, is in good taste. The pattern is in 8 sizes for girls from 5 to 12 years old. For a girl of 8 years, the coat needs 5⅝ yards of goods 22 inches wide, or 2⅞ yards 44 inches wide, or 2¼ yards 54 inches wide. Price of pattern, 1s. 3d. or 30 cents.

No. 4716.—LITTLE BOYS' FAUNTLEROY COSTUME. —By referring to figure No. 395 A on page 94 of this issue, this costume may be again seen. The pattern is in 6 sizes for little boys from 2 to 7 years of age. To make the costume for a boy of 3 years, will require 2⅛ yards of velvet 20 inches wide, or 1⅝ yard 27 inches wide, each with 1 yard of cambric 36 inches wide, ⅜ yard of all-over embroidery 27 inches wide, and 2¼ yards of silk. Price of pattern, 1s. or 25 cents.

4716   **4716**

FIGURE NO. 337 A.—BRIDE'S TOILETTE.- This consists of Ladies' basque No. 4701 (copyright), shown again on page 89; and skirt No. 4734 (copyright), on page 88. The basque pattern is in 13 sizes for ladies from 28 to 46 inches, bust measure, and costs 1s. 3d. or 30 cents. The skirt pattern is in 9 sizes for ladies from 20 to 36 inches, waist measure, and costs 1s. 8d. or 40 cents. To make the toilette for a lady of medium size, will require 6½ yards of material 44 inches wide: the skirt needing 4½ yards; and the basque, 2 yards.

No. 4710.—BOYS' DOUBLE-BREASTED OVER-COAT, BUTTONED TO THE THROAT.—This pattern is in 8 sizes for boys from 3 to 10 years of age. For a boy of 7 years, it needs 2¾ yds. of goods 27 inches wide, or 1⅜ yd. 54 inches wide. Price of pattern, 1s. or 25 cents.

4710

4710

FIGURE NO. 374 A.—MISSES' RUSSIAN COAT.—This portrays Misses' Russian coat No. 4674 (copyright), shown again on page 89 of this issue. Gray cloth and Bengaline were united in the construction of this coat, with charming effect. The pattern is in 7 sizes for misses from 10 to 16 years of age, and costs 1s. 3d. or 30 cents. To make the garment of one material for a miss of 12 years, requires 5 yards 22 inches wide, or 2⅜ yards 44 inches wide, or 1⅞ yard 54 inches wide.

4712

4712

No. 4712.—BOYS' NORFOLK JACKET.—The pattern of this comfortable jacket is in 7 sizes for boys from 3 to 9 years of age. For a boy of 7 years, it needs 2¾ yards of goods 27 inches wide. If material 54 inches wide be chosen, 1⅜ yard will prove sufficient. Price of pattern, 10d. or 20 cents.

· FIGURE NO. 380 A.—GIRLS' DRESS.—This is Girls' dress No. 4663 (copyright), shown on page 94. The pattern is in 8 sizes for girls from 5 to 12 years of age, and costs 1s. or 25 cents. For a girl of 8 years, it requires 5⅝ yards of goods 22 inches wide, or 2¾ yards 44 inches wide. In the combination shown on page 94, it needs 3⅜ yards of goods 40 inches wide, and ⅞ yard of silk.

FIGURE NO. 353 A.—LADIES' COSTUME.—This represents Ladies' costume No. 4678 (copyright), again seen on page 86. The pattern is in 13 sizes for ladies from 28 to 46 inches, bust measure, and costs 1s. 8d. or 40 cents. Of one material for a lady of medium size, it requires 11 yards 22 inches wide, or 5¾ yards 44 inches wide, or 4⅝ yards 50 inches wide.

No. 4698.—MISSES' VEST (Copyright).—The pattern of the pretty vest here shown is in 7 sizes for misses from 10 to 16 years of age. To make the garment for a miss of 12 years, calls for 1¼ yard of material 20 inches wide, or 1 yard 30 inches wide, or ⅞ yard 44 inches wide. Price of pattern, 7d. or 15 cents.

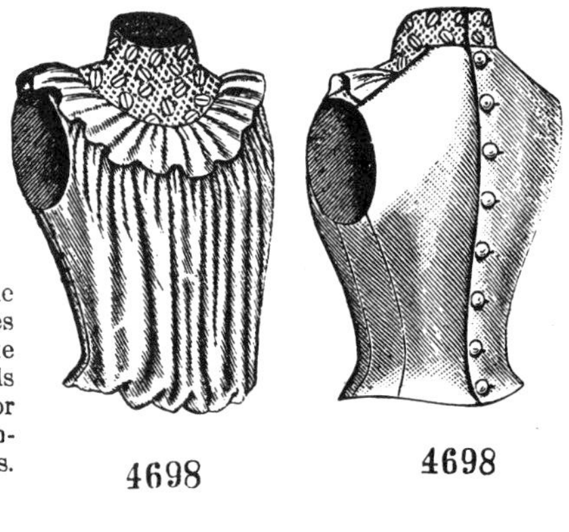

4698

4698

No. 4688.—LITTLE GIRLS' RUSSIAN CLOAK (Copyright).—At figure No. 392 A on page 94 this charming little cloak is again portrayed. Cashmere was chosen for the garment in this instance, and feather trimming provides the garniture. The pattern is in 9 sizes for little girls from 1 to 9 years of age. To make the garment for a girl of 5 years, requires 5 yards of goods 22 inches wide, or 2⅝ yards 44 inches wide, or 2⅜ yards 54 inches wide. Price of pattern, 10d. or 20 cents.

4688   4688

FIGURE No. 359 A.—LADIES' MARGUERITE WAIST.—This is Ladies' basque No. 4683 (copyright), shown again on page 89. The pattern is in 13 sizes for ladies from 28 to 46 inches, bust measure, and costs 1s. 3d. or 30 cents. For a lady of medium size, it requires 4¾ yards of goods 22 inches wide, or 3⅜ yards 30 inches wide, or 2¾ yards 44 inches wide.

4706

No. 4706.—BOYS' VEST, WITH SHAWL COLLAR.—The pattern of this stylishly devised vest is in 14 sizes for boys from 3 to 16 years old. To make the garment for a boy of 11 years, needs ¾ yard of goods 27 ins. wide, or ⅝ yard 54 ins. wide. Price of pattern, 7d. or 15 cts.

FIGURE No. 346 A.—LADIES' HOUSE COSTUME.—This depicts Ladies' Russian Princess costume No. 4684 (copyr't), again seen on page 86. The pattern is in 13 sizes for ladies from 28 to 46 inches, bust measure, and costs 1s. 8d. or 40 cents. Of one material for a lady of medium size, it requires 10¾ yards 22 inches wide, or 6 yards 44 inches wide.

FIGURE No. 381 A.—MISSES' JACKET.—This depicts Misses' jacket No. 4682 (copyright), shown again on page 91. The pattern is in 9 sizes for misses from 8 to 16 years of age, and costs 1s. or 25 cents. For a miss of 12 years, the jacket needs 4⅛ yards of material 22 inches wide, or 2 yards 44 inches wide, or 1⅝ yard 54 inches wide.

43

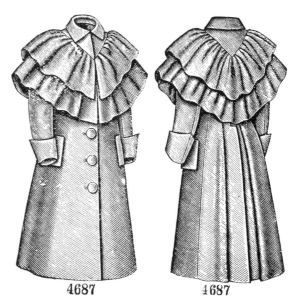

No. 4687.—GIRLS' LONG COAT (Copyright).—This pattern, also shown at figure No. 385 A on page 84, is in 10 sizes for girls from 3 to 12 years of age. For a girl of 8 years, it needs 6½ yards of goods 22 inches wide, or 3¼ yards 44 inches wide. Price of pattern, 1s. 3d. or 30 cents.

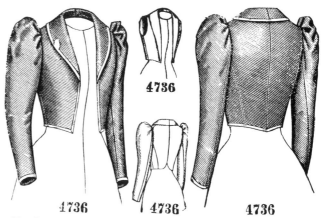

No. 4736.—MISSES' ETON JACKET (Copyright).—This jacket is again illustrated at figure No. 382 A on page 89. It is here shown made of dress goods and bound with braid. The pattern is in 7 sizes for misses from 10 to 16 years of age. To make the jacket for a miss of 12 years, needs 2½ yards of material 22 inches wide, or 1¼ yard 44 inches wide, or 1⅛ yard 54 inches wide. Price of pattern, 7d. or 15 cents.

FIGURE NO. 368 A.—LADIES' WATTEAU COAT.—This represents Ladies' Watteau coat No. 4677 (copyright), shown again on page 88. The pattern is in 13 sizes for ladies from 28 to 46 inches, bust measure, and costs 1s. 6d. or 35 cents. For a lady of medium size, it requires 7⅜ yards of material 22 inches wide, or 3½ yards 44 inches wide, or 3 yards 54 inches wide.

No. 4690.—MISSES' AND GIRLS' TRIPLE CAPE (Copyright).—This cape is prettily illustrated made of plain cloth and finished with a row of machine-stitching. It may be made up as a stylish addition to a tailor-made gown when developed in cheviot, smooth-surfaced cloth or any suitable material. The pattern is in 7 sizes from 4 to 16 years of age. To make the garment for a miss of 12 years, will require 2⅞ yards of material 22 inches wide, or 1⅝ yard 44 inches wide, or 1½ yard 54 inches wide. Price of pattern, 7d. or 15 cents.

No. 4686.—GIRLS' DRESS (TO BE WORN WITH A GUIMPE) (Copyright).—This pattern is in 10 sizes for girls from 3 to 12 years old. To make the dress for a girl of 8 years, requires 5⅞ yards of goods 22 inches wide, or 4¾ yards 27 inches wide, or 3⅞ yards 36 inches wide. If material 44 inches wide be selected, then 3¼ yards will prove sufficient. Price of pattern, 10d. or 20 cents.

FIGURE NO. 366 A.—LADIES' ULSTER.—This illustrates Ladies' ulster No. 4727 (copyright), which is again depicted on page 87. A full-length back view of the garment is given at figure No. 367 A on page 91. The pattern is in 13 sizes for ladies from 28 to 46 inches, bust measure, and costs 1s. 8d. or 40 cents. For a lady of medium size, it requires 8⅝ yards of material 22 inches wide, or 4⅞ yards 44 inches wide, or 3⅝ yards 54 inches wide, each with ⅞ yard of silk 20 inches wide to line the hood.

FIGURE NO. 370 A.—LADIES' COAT.—This portrays Ladies' coat No. 4695 (copyright), again shown on page 90. The pattern is in 13 sizes for ladies from 28 to 46 inches, bust measure, and costs 1s. 6d. or 35 cents. For a lady of medium size, it requires 6¾ yards of goods 22 inches wide, or 4¾ yards 44 inches wide, or 3⅝ yards 54 inches wide.

FIGURE NO. 373 A. — MISSES' JACKET. —- This illustrates Misses' jacket No. 4682 (copyright). which is again portrayed on page 91. The pattern is in 9 sizes for misses from 8 to 16 years of age, and costs 1s. or 25 cents. To make the garment for a miss of 12 years, will require 4⅛ yards of material 22 inches wide, or 2 yards 44 inches wide. If 54-inch-wide goods be selected, then 1⅝ yard will prove sufficient.

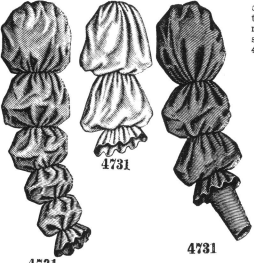

4731

4731

4731

NO. 4731.—LADIES' DRESS SLEEVE (WITH FITTED LINING) (TO BE MADE WITH TWO, THREE OR FIVE PUFFS) (Copyright).—This pattern is in 7 sizes for ladies from 9 to 15 ins., arm measure, measuring the arm about an inch below the bottom of the arm's-eye. For a lady whose arm measures 11 inches as described, a pair of sleeves needs 3⅛ yards of goods **22 inches wide. Price of pattern, 5d. or 10 cents.**

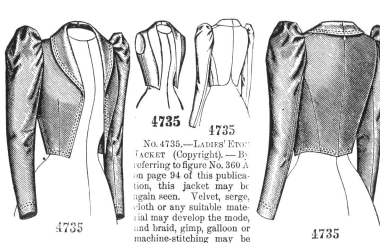

4735

4735

4735

4735

NO. 4735.—LADIES' ETON JACKET (Copyright). — By referring to figure No. 360 A on page 94 of this publication, this jacket may be again seen. Velvet, serge, cloth or any suitable material may develop the mode, and braid, gimp, galloon or machine-stitching may be used to trim. The pattern is in 13 sizes for ladies from 28 to 46 inches, bust measure. For a lady of medium size, it will need 3 yards of goods 22 inches wide, or 1½ yard 44 inches wide. Of material 54 inches wide, 1¼ yard will prove sufficient. Price of pattern, 10d. or 20 cents.

4671

4671

4693

No. 4693.—LADIES' ORNAMENTAL BELTS (Copyr't).—One of these belts is shown at figure No. 360 A on page 94. The pattern is in 9 sizes for ladies from 20 to 36 ins., waist measure. For a lady of medium size, the round belt needs ½ yd. of goods 20 ins. or more wide. The belt with pointed lower edge requires ⅝ yard 20 inches or more wide, while that having pointed ends needs ⅝ yard 20 inches wide. Price, 5d. or 10 cts.

No. 4671.—CHILD'S DRESS (Copyright).— This pattern, also shown at figure No. 394 A on page 92, is in 7 sizes for children from ½ to 6 years of age. For a child of 5 years, it needs 2½ yds. of nainsook 36 inches wide, with ¼ yard of all-over embroidery 27 inches wide. Of one material, it needs 3¾ yards 22 inches wide, or 3 yards 27 inches wide, or 2¼ yards 36 inches wide. Price, 10d. or 20 cents.

FIGURE NO. 361 A.—LADIES' TOILETTE. — This consists of Ladies' Eton jacket No. 4634 (copyright), shown on page 82; and Empire vest No. 4696 (copyright), on page 89. The jacket pattern is in 13 sizes for ladies from 28 to 46 inches, bust measure, and costs 1s. or 25 cents. The vest pattern is in 13 sizes for ladies from 28 to 46 inches, bust measure, and costs 10d. or 20 cents. Of goods 44 inches wide for a lady of medium size, the vest will require ⅞ yard, and the jacket, 1⅝ yard.

No. 4711. BOYS' ULSTER (TO BE WORN WITH OR WITHOUT A HOOD).— This ulster may be developed in both smooth and rough surfaced coatings, with machine-stitching for an edge finish. The pattern is in 10 sizes for boys from 3 to 12 years of age. For a boy of 7 years, it needs 3½ yards of goods 27 inches wide, or 1¾ yard 54 inches wide. Price of pattern, 1s. or 25 cents.

4711

4711

FIGURE NO. 357 A.—LADIES' PROMENADE TOILETTE.—This consists of Ladies' bell skirt No. 4694 (copyr't), seen on page 93; and blouse-waist No. 4192 (copyr't), on page 12. The skirt pattern is in 9 sizes for ladies from 20 to 36 ins., waist meas., and costs 1s. 6d. or 35 cts. The waist pattern is in 13 sizes for ladies from 28 to 46 ins., bust meas., and costs 1s. 3d. or 30 cts. For goods needed, see pages 12 and 9.

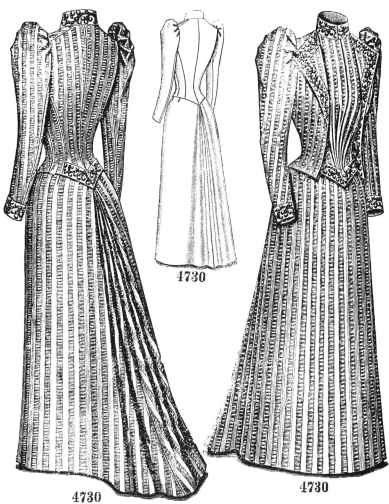

4730

4730

4730

No. 4730.—LADIES' COSTUME, WITH ETON JACKET FRONTS, AND A SLIGHT TRAIN (PERFORATED FOR ROUND LENGTH) (Copyright).—At figures Nos. 342 A and 344 A on pages 87 and 91 this costume is again represented. The pattern is in 13 sizes for ladies from 28 to 46 inches, bust measure. To make the costume for a lady of medium size, will need 9¼ yards of goods 22 inches wide, or 4⅞ yards 44 inches wide, or 4½ yards 50 inches wide. Price of pattern, 1s. 8d. or 40 cents.

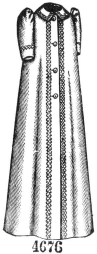

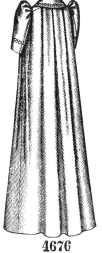

No. 4676.—INFANTS' WRAPPER (Copyright).—This comfortable little gown may be made up very prettily in flannel, and feather-stitching wrought in embroidery silk will trim it effectively. Any soft woollen material may be developed by the mode. The pattern is in one size, and, to make a garment like it,

4676

4676

needs 2⅞ yards of goods 27 inches wide, or 2⅛ yards of material 36 inches wide. Price of pattern, 10d. or 20 cts.

FIGURE NO. 358 A.—LADIES' COSTUME.—This represents Ladies' costume No. 4724 (copyright). shown again on page 87. *Plissé* wool goods, velvet and all-over Russian embroidery are united in this instance, and jewelled Russian embroidered bands provide the trimming. The pattern is in 13 sizes for ladies from 28 to 46 inches, bust measure, and costs 1s. 8d. or 40 cents. To make the costume for a lady of medium size, will require 11¼ yards of material 22 inches wide, or 5⅝ yards 44 inches wide, or 4⅞ yards 50 inches wide.

No. 4664.—Misses' Costume (Copyright).—At figure No. 379 A on page 91 this stylish costume is again represented. The pattern is in 7 sizes for misses from 10 to 16 years old. As pictured for a miss of 12 years, it calls for 3 yards of checked and 1¼ yard of plain cheviot 40 inches wide. Of one material, it needs 6¾ yards 22 inches wide, or 3⅜ yards 44 inches wide, or 3 yards 50 inches wide. Price of pattern, 1s. 6d. or 35 cents.

Figure No. 342 A.—Ladies' Costume.—This illustrates Ladies' costume No. 4730 (copyright), again portrayed on page 86. The pattern is in 13 sizes for ladies from 28 to 46 inches, bust measure, and costs 1s. 8d. or 40 cents. Of one material for a lady of medium size, it needs 9¼ yards 22 inches wide, or 4⅞ yards 44 inches wide, or 4½ yards 50 inches wide.

No. 4724.—Ladies' Costume, with a Short Train (Perforated for Round Length) (Copyr't).—This pattern, also shown at figure No. 358 A on page 86, is in 13 sizes for ladies from 28 to 46 inches, bust measure. For a lady of medium size, it needs 11¼ yards of goods 22 ins. wide, or 5⅝ yards 44 ins. wide, or 4⅞ yards 50 inches wide. Price, 1s. 8d. or 40 cts.

No. 4721.—Ladies' Long Basque (Known as the Norfolk Jacket) (Copyr't).—At figure No. 363 A on page 90 this basque is again shown. The pattern is in 13 sizes for ladies from 28 to 46 inches, bust measure. For a lady of medium size, it needs 5¾ yards of goods 22 inches wide, or 2⅞ yards 44 inches wide, or 2½ yards 54 inches wide. Price of pattern, 1s. 3d. or 30 cents.

No. 4680.—Ladies' Princess Dress, with Slight Train (Perforated for Round Length) (Also Known as the Parthenia Gown) (Copyright).—This dress is again shown at figure No. 347 A on page 89, and will develop handsomely in brocade, Bengaline, faille, cloth, camel's-hair or serge, with beaded net, passementerie, embroidered bands or heavy laces for decoration. The pattern is in 13 sizes for ladies from 28 to 46 inches, bust measure. To make the dress for a lady of medium size, will require 12⅜ yards of goods 22 inches wide, or 6⅞ yards 44 inches wide, or 5⅞ yards 50 inches wide. Price of pattern, 1s. 8d. or 40 cents.

Figure No. 343 A.—Ladies' Costume.—This represents Ladies' costume No. 4723 (copyright), again depicted on page 86. The pattern is in 13 sizes for ladies from 28 to 46 inches, bust measure, and costs 1s. 8d. or 40 cents. For a lady of medium size, it requires 11¾ yards of material 22 inches wide, or 6 yards 44 inches wide, or 5½ yards 50 inches wide.

49

4669

4669

4669

4704

4704

No. 4704.—
Boys' Long
Overcoat,
with Cape.—
The comfort-
able garment
here pic-
tured will
make up at-
tractively in
all seasonable
varieties of
wool goods
in vogue. The
pattern is
in 14 sizes for
boys from 3 to
16 years of
age. For a boy
of 11 years,
the overcoat requires 6 yards of material 27 inches wide, or 3
yards 54 inches wide. Price of pattern, 1s. 3d. or 30 cents.

No. 4669.—Ladies' Costume, with Skirt Adjusted Over the Lower Edge of
the Basque, and Having a Slight Train (Perforated for Round Length)
(Copyright).—Another view of this costume is given at figure No. 356 A on page 92.
The yoke facing may be omitted, as illustrated in the small engraving. The pattern
is in 13 sizes for ladies from 28 to 46 inches, bust measure. To make the costume
for a lady of medium size, needs 8 yards of goods 22 inches wide, or 4¼ yards
44 inches wide, or 4 yards 50 inches wide. Price of pattern, 1s. 8d. or 40 cents

4677

4677

No. 4677.—Ladies' Watteau Coat (Copyright).—This pattern, again
shown at figure No. 368 A on page 85, is in 13 sizes for ladies from 28 to 46
inches, bust measure. For a lady of medium size, it needs 7⅜ yards of material
22 inches wide, or 3½ yards 44 inches wide. Price of pattern, 1s. 6d. or 35 cts.

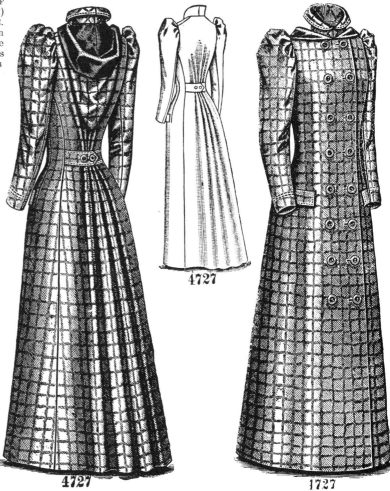

4727

4727

4727

4727

No. 4727.—Ladies' Ulster (To be Made With or Without a Hood) (Copyright).—Other views of this stylish garment are presented at figures Nos. 366 A and
367 A on pages 85 and 91. The pattern is in 13 sizes for ladies from 28 to 46 inches,
bust measure. For a lady of medium size, it requires 8⅝ yards of material 22 inches
wide, or 4⅞ yards 44 inches wide, or 3⅝ yards 54 inches wide. In each instance, ⅞ yard
of silk 20 inches wide will be needed to line the hood. Price of pattern, 1s. 8d. or 40 cts.

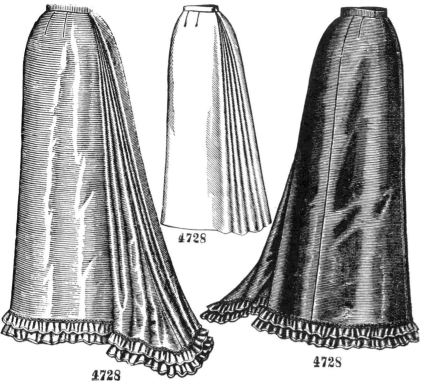

4728

No. 4728.—Ladies' Bell Skirt, with Fitted Front-Gore, and a Slight Train (Perforated for Round Length) (Copyright).—This skirt is again represented at figures Nos. 338 A, 339 A and 352 A on pages 89, 92 and 93. The pattern is in 9 sizes for ladies from 20 to 36 inches, waist measure. For a lady of medium size, it needs $6\frac{1}{8}$ yards of goods 22 inches wide, or $3\frac{3}{4}$ yards 44 ins. wide, or $3\frac{1}{8}$ yds. 50 ins. wide. Price, 1s. 6d. or 35 cents.

4684

No. 4684.—Ladies' Russian Princess Costume, with Slight Train (Perforated for Round Length) (Copyright).—This pattern, which is again illustrated at figure No. 346 A on page 85, is in 13 sizes for ladies from 28 to 46 inches, bust measure. For a lady of medium size, it requires $10\frac{3}{4}$ yards of material 22 inches wide, or 6 yards 44 inches wide. In the combination represented, the costume calls for 6 yards of cashmere 40 inches wide, with 2 yards of silk 20 inches wide. Price of pattern, 1s. 8d. or 40 cents.

Figure No. 354 A.—Ladies' Promenade Toilette.—This consists of Ladies' Russian coat No. 4665 (copyr't), shown on page 91; and bell skirt No. 3967 (copyr't), on page 37. The coat pattern is in 13 sizes for ladies from 28 to 46 ins., bust meas.; the skirt pattern is in 9 sizes for ladies from 20 to 36 ins., waist meas., and each costs 1s. 6d. or 35 cts. Of goods 44 inches wide for a lady of medium size, the coat needs $3\frac{5}{8}$ yards, and the skirt $3\frac{1}{2}$ yards, with $6\frac{3}{4}$ yards of silk for the foundation skirt and a ruffle.

51

4679

4679   **4679**

No. 4679. — Ladies' Double-Breasted Watteau Coat (Copyright). —This coat is also shown at figure No. 339 A on page 92. The pattern is in 13 sizes for ladies from 28 to 46 inches, bust measure. For a lady of medium size, it needs 7 yards of goods 22 inches wide, or 3½ yards 44 inches wide, or 2⅞ yards 54 inches wide. Price of pattern, 1s. 6d. or 35 cents.

Figure No. 340 A.—Ladies' Russian Toilette.—This consists of Ladies' Russian blouse No. 4689 (copyright), shown again on page 91; and circular bell skirt No. 4482 (copyright), on page 35. The blouse pattern is in 13 sizes for ladies from 28 to 46 inches, bust measure, and costs 1s. 3d. or 30 cents. The skirt pattern is in 9 sizes for ladies from 20 to 36 inches, waist measure, and costs 1s. 6d. or 35 cents. Of goods 44 inches wide for a lady of medium size, the toilette needs 6⅜ yards.

Figure No. 389 A. — Child's Coat.—This portrays Child's coat No. 4668 (copyr't), shown on page 90. The pattern is in 7 sizes for children from ½ to 6 years of age, and costs 10d. or 20 cents. For a child of 5 years, the coat will require 5 yards of material 22 inches wide, or 2½ yards 44 inches wide, or 2¼ yards 54 inches wide.

Figure No. 390 A.—Little Girls' Cloak —This illustrates Little Girls' cloak No. 4681 (copyright), again portrayed on page 94. The pattern is in 6 sizes for little girls from 1 to 6 years of age, and costs 10d. or 20 cents. To make the garment for a girl of 5 years, will require 5⅞ yards of material 22 inches wide, or 3¼ yards 44 inches wide, or 2⅝ yards 54 inches wide.

FIGURE No. 351 A.—LADIES' STREET
TOILETTE.—This consists of Ladies' skirt
No. 4700 (copyright), depicted on page 92;
and basque No. 4702 (copyright), on page
89. The skirt pattern is in 9 sizes for
ladies from 20 to 36 inches, waist measure,
and costs 1s. 6d. or 35 cents. The basque
pattern is in 13 sizes for ladies from 28
to 46 inches, bust measure, and costs
1s. 3d. or 30 cents. For a lady of medium
size, the skirt needs 6¾ yards, and the
basque 4⅝ yards, of goods 22 inches wide.

4734

4734

FIGURE No. 378 A.—MISSES' OUTDOOR
TOILETTE. — This consists of Misses' bell
skirt No. 4697 (copyright), shown on page
93; and blouse-waist No. 4223 (copyright),
on page 52. The skirt pattern is in 7 sizes
for misses from 10 to 16 years of age, and
costs 1s. 3d. or 30 cents. The waist pattern
is in 7 sizes for misses from 10 to 16 years
old, and costs 1s. or 25 cents. Of goods 44
inches wide for a miss of 12 years, the skirt
needs 1⅝ yard, and the waist, 2⅛ yards.

4734

No. 4734.—LADIES' LONG–TRAINED SKIRT (PERFORATED FOR POINTED AND THREE-
QUARTER TRAIN) (Copyright).—This pattern, again represented at figure No. 337 A on
page 84, is in 9 sizes for ladies from 20 to 36 inches, waist measure. To make the
skirt for a lady of medium size, will require 8⅛ yards of material 22 inches wide, or
4½ yards either 44 or 50 inches wide. Price of pattern, 1s. 8d. or 40 cents.

53

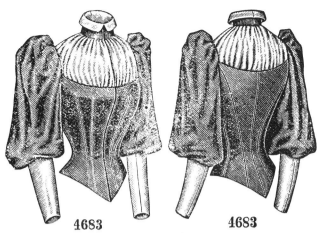

4683   **4683**

No. 4683.—LADIES' BASQUE (ALSO KNOWN AS THE MARGUERITE WAIST) (Copyr't).—This pattern, also shown at figure No. 359 A on page 85, is in 13 sizes for ladies from 28 to 46 inches, bust measure. For a lady of medium size, it needs 1⅞ yard of dress goods 40 inches wide, and 2⅜ yards of silk 20 inches wide. Price of pattern, 1s. 3d. or 30 cents.

FIGURE No. 398 A. — LITTLE BOYS' SUIT.—This consists of Little Boys' costume No. 4708, shown on page 91; and cap No. 3033, on page 66. For sizes, prices, and materials required, see pages 66 and 91.

FIGURE No. 399 A.—LITTLE BOYS' SUIT.—This consists of Little Boys' overcoat No. 4707, and kilt skirt No. 4718 (copyright), both shown on page 94; and cap No. 3033, on page 66. For sizes, prices, and goods needed, see pages 66 and 94.

FIGURE No. 382 A.—MISSES' PROMENADE TOILETTE.—This consists of Misses' Eton jacket No. 4736 (copyr't), shown on page 84; corselet Princess skirt No. 4725 (copyright), on page 91; and blouse-waist No. 4223 (copyright), on page 52. For sizes, prices, and materials needed, see pages 52, 84 and 91.

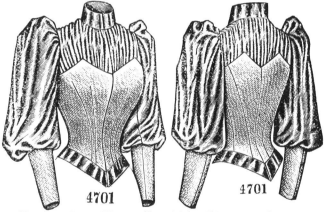

4701   **4701**

No. 4701.—LADIES' BASQUE (Copyright).—This pattern, also shown at figure 337 A on page 84, is in 13 sizes for ladies from 28 to 46 inches, bust measure. As pictured for a lady of medium size, it requires 1 yard of dress goods 40 inches wide, and 2⅞ yards of silk. Of one material, it needs 3⅜ yards 22 inches wide, or 2 yards 44 inches wide. Price of pattern, 1s. 3d. or 30 cents.

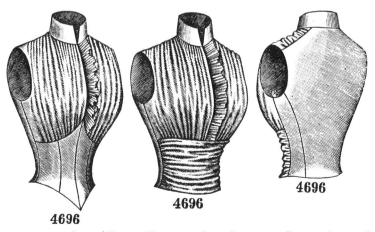

4696   **4696**   **4696**

No. 4696.—LADIES' EMPIRE VEST, WITH SASH-GIRDLE AND POINTED GIRDLE (Copyright).—This vest is again portrayed at figure No. 361 A on page 86. It may be developed in India, China or wash silk or any soft, pliable material. The pattern is in 13 sizes for ladies from 28 to 46 inches, bust measure. To make the garment for a lady of medium size, requires 1⅞ yard of goods 22 inches wide, or 1 yard 36 inches wide, or ⅞ yard 44 inches wide, or ¾ yard 50 inches wide. Price of pattern, 10d. or 20 cents.

No. 4714.—Boys' Pea-Jacket.—The pattern of this comfortable jacket is in 12 sizes for boys from 5 to 16 years of age. For a boy of 11 years, it requires 2⅝ yards of material 27 inches wide, or 1⅜ yard 54 inches wide. Price of pattern, 1s. or 25 cents.

No. 4717.—Little Boys' Russian Suit. — At figure No. 396 A on page 93 this suit is again portrayed. The pattern is in 6 sizes for little boys from 2 to 7 years of age, and will develop attractively in serge, flannel, outing cloth or any similar material. To make the suit for a boy of 5 years, needs 3⅜ yards of goods 27 inches wide, or 1¾ yard of material 54 inches wide. Price of pattern, 1s. or 25 cts.

No. 4713.—Boys' Sack Coat, Buttoning to the Neck.—This pattern is in 14 sizes for boys from 3 to 16 years old. For a boy of 11 years, it needs 2¾ yards of goods 27 inches wide, or 1⅜ yard 54 inches wide. Price of pattern, 1s. or 25 cents.

Figure No. 347 A.—Ladies' Visiting Dress.—This is Ladies' Princess dress No. 4680 (copyright), again shown on page 87. The pattern is in 13 sizes for ladies from 28 to 46 inches, bust measure, and costs 1s. 8d. or 40 cents. To make the dress of one material for a lady of medium size, will require 12⅜ yards 22 inches wide, or 6⅞ yards 44 inches wide, or 5⅞ yards 50 inches wide.

Figure No. 338 A.—Ladies' Visiting Toilette.—This consists of Ladies' bell skirt No. 4728 (copyr't), shown on page 88; and basque No. 4733 (copyr't), on page 92. The skirt pattern is in 9 sizes for ladies from 20 to 36 inches, waist meas., and costs 1s. 6d. or 35 cents. The basque pattern is in 13 sizes for ladies from 28 to 46 inches, bust meas., and costs 1s. 3d. or 30 cents. For a lady of medium size, they need 9⅞ yards of goods 22 inches wide.

4674

4674

No. 4674.—
Misses' Russian
Coat (Copyr't).—
Another view of
this garment is
given at figure
No. 374 A on
page 85. Gray
mixed cheviot
was here chosen

4674

for the coat, and machine-stitching and buttons provide a stylish finish. The pattern is in 7 sizes for misses from 10 to 16 years of age. For a miss of 12 years, the coat needs 5 yards of material 22 inches wide, or 2⅜ yards 44 inches wide. If goods 54 inches wide be used, 1⅞ yard will suffice. Price of pattern, 1s. 3d. or 30 cts.

4685

4685

No. 4685.—Misses' Dress (Copyright).—This dress is also shown at figure No. 376 A on this page. The pattern is in 9 sizes for misses from 8 to 16 years of age. For a miss of 12 years, the dress requires 3⅛ yards of cashmere 40 inches wide, with 2⅝ yards of silk 20 inches wide. Of one material, it calls for 6¾ yards 22 inches wide, or 3⅝ yards 44 inches wide. Price, 1s. 3d or 30 cts.

4703

4703

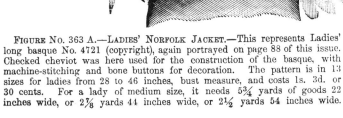

Figure No. 363 A.—Ladies' Norfolk Jacket.—This represents Ladies' long basque No. 4721 (copyright), again portrayed on page 88 of this issue. Checked cheviot was here used for the construction of the basque, with machine-stitching and bone buttons for decoration. The pattern is in 13 sizes for ladies from 28 to 46 inches, bust measure, and costs 1s. 3d. or 30 cents. For a lady of medium size, it needs 5¾ yards of goods 22 inches wide, or 2⅞ yards 44 inches wide, or 2½ yards 54 inches wide.

No. 4703. — Ladies' Wrap (Copyright).—This wrap is again portrayed at figure No. 362 A on page 93. The pattern is in 10 sizes for ladies from 28 to 46 inches, bust measure, and may be developed in cloth, velvet, silk or any cloaking, with galloon, passementerie, etc., for trimming. In the combination shown for a lady of medium size, it needs ⅝ yard of coarse lace net 27 inches wide, 2¼ yards of lace flouncing 23 inches wide, and ¾ yard of lace flouncing 45¾ inches wide. Of one material, it requires 4¾ yards 22 inches wide, or 2⅝ yards 44 inches wide, or 2 yards 54 inches wide. Price of pattern, 1s. 3d. or 30 cents.

56

4666

4666   **4666**

No. 4666.—LADIES' LONG WRAP (TO BE MADE WITH OR WITHOUT A HOOD) (Copyright).—By referring to figure No. 365 A on page 92, this wrap may be again observed. Fancy cloaking and silk were here used for the wrap, and a plain finish is observed. Broadcloth, camel's-hair, Bedford cord, beaver, kersey, etc., will also make up stylishly by this mode. The pattern is in 10 sizes for ladies from 28 to 46 inches, bust measure. For a lady of medium size, the wrap calls for 3⅜ yards of fancy cloaking 54 inches wide, with 1⅛ yard of silk 20 inches wde. Of one material, it needs 4 yards 44 inches wide, or 3⅜ yards 54 inches wide. Price of pattern, 1s. 8d. or 40 cts.

4672   **4672**

4672

No. 4672.—LADIES' RUSSIAN BLOUSE (WITH FITTED LININGS) (Copyright).—This stylish garment is again shown at figures Nos. 341 A and 318 A on page 94. It may be developed in any fashionable variety of silk, wool or cotton goods, with feather trimming, galloon or passementerie for garniture. The pattern is in 13 sizes for ladies from 28 to 46 inches, bust measure. For a lady of medium size, it needs 5½ yards of goods 22 inches wide, or 3 yards 44 inches wide, or 2¾ yards 50 inches wide. Price of pattern, 1s. 3d. or 30 cents.

FIGURE NO. 364 A.—LADIES' PROMENADE TOILETTE.—This consists of Ladies' cape No. 4675 (copyright), which is again pictured on page 94; and skirt No. 4373 (copyright), shown on page 35. The cape pattern is in 10 sizes for ladies from 28 to 46 inches, bust measure, and costs 1s. 6d. or 35 cents. The skirt pattern is in 9 sizes for ladies from 20 to 36 inches, waist measure, and costs 1s. 6d. or 35 cents. Of material 44 inches wide for a lady of medium size, the skirt needs 2⅞ yards; and the cape, 3⅞ yards.

57

NO. 4708.— LITTLE BOYS' COSTUME.— This trim little costume is again represented at figure No. 398 A on page 89. Any appropriate material, such as cheviot, serge, cloth or tweed will make up with pleasing and stylish effect, and the finish may, if desired, be plain. The pattern is in 6 sizes for little boys from 2 to 7 years of age. To make the costume for a boy of 5 years, requires 3½ yards of material 27 inches wide, or 1¾ yard 54 inches wide. Price of pattern, 1s. or 25 cents.

4708

4708

NO. 4699.— MISSES' COAT, WITH WATTEAU BACK (IN THREE-QUARTER LENGTH) (Copyright). — This coat is also shown at figure No. 372 A on this page. Striped cloth is here pictured in the garment, and machine-stitching provides a neat completion. The pattern is in 9 sizes for misses from 8 to 16 years of age. To make the garment for a miss of 12 years, needs 4¾ yards of material 22 inches wide, or 2½ yards 44 inches wide, or 2 yards 54 inches wide. Price of pattern, 1s. 3d. or 30 cts.

4699

4699

4668

4668

NO. 4668.— CHILD'S COAT (WITH BODY AND SLEEVE LININGS) (Copyright).— This pattern, also shown at figure No. 389 A on page 88, is in 7 sizes for children from ½ to 6 years old. To make the coat for a child of 5 years, needs 5 yards of material 22 inches wide, or 2½ yards 44 inches wide, or 2¼ yards 54 inches wide. Price, 10d. or 20 cts.

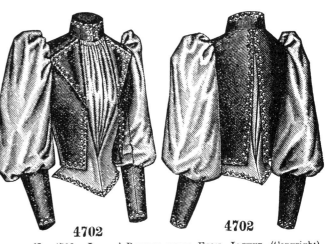

4702

4702

FIGURE NO. 376 A.— MISSES' DRESS.— This represents Misses' dress No. 4685 (copyright), again shown on this page. The pattern is in 9 sizes for misses from 8 to 16 years of age, and costs 1s. 3d. or 30 cents. To make the dress for a miss of 12 years, requires 6¾ yards of material 22 inches wide, or 3⅝ yards 44 inches wide. In the combination pictured elsewhere on this page, it needs 3⅛ yards of cashmere 40 inches wide, with 2⅝ yards of silk.

FIGURE NO. 377 A.— MISSES' JOSEPHINE DRESS.— This illustrates Misses' Josephine or Empire dress No. 4691 (copyright), again shown on page 92. White India silk was here chosen for the dress, and ribbon trims it. The pattern is in 9 sizes for misses from 8 to 16 years of age, and costs 1s. 3d. or 30 cents. For a miss of 12 years, it needs 7⅛ yards of goods 22 inches wide, or 5⅜ yards 30 inches wide, or 3⅞ yards 44 inches wide.

NO. 4702.— LADIES' BASQUE, WITH ETON JACKET (Copyright).— Other views of this garment are given at figures Nos. 351 A and 350 A on pages 88 and 91. The pattern is in 13 sizes for ladies from 28 to 46 inches, bust measure. For a lady of medium size, it needs 4⅝ yards of goods 22 inches wide, or 2⅜ yards 44 inches wide. In the combination illustrated, it calls for 1⅛ yard of dark and 1⅞ yard of light goods each 40 inches wide. Price of pattern, 1s. 3d. or 30 cents.

4732 **4732**

NO. 4732.—LADIES' RUSSIAN REEFER JACKET (Copyright).—
Another view of this stylish garment is represented at figure No.
369 A on page 93. Smooth-faced coating is here pictured in the
jacket, and machine-stitching forms the completion. Any suitable
coating will develop nicely by the mode. The pattern is in 13
sizes for ladies from 28 to 46 inches, bust measure. To make
the jacket for a lady of medium size, will require 5¼ yards of
material 22 inches wide, or 2⅝ yards 44 inches wide, or 2¼
yards 54 inches wide. Price of pattern, 1s. 3d. or 30 cents.

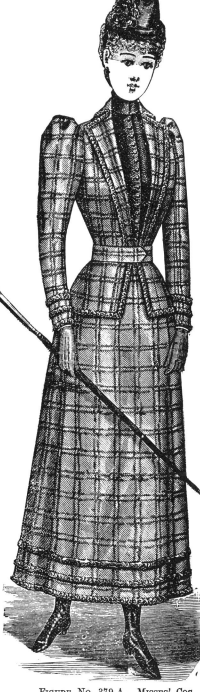

4673 **4673**

NO. 4673.—LITTLE GIRLS'
DRESS (TO BE WORN WITH
A GUIMPE) (Copyright). —
Another view of this quaint
little gown is shown at figure No. 391 A on page 94.
Figured challis was chosen
for the dress in this instance,
and baby ribbon supplies
the trimming. Gingham,
percale, lawn, silk, cashmere or any soft, pliable
material will make up effectively in this way. The pattern is in 5 sizes for little
girls from 2 to 6 years of age.
To make the dress for a girl
of 5 years, will require 4⅜
yards of material 22 inches
wide, or 3⅜ yards 30 in-
ches wide, or 2⅜ yards
44 inches wide. Price of
pattern, 10d. or 20 cents.

FIGURE NO. 379 A.—MISSES' COS-
TUME.—This portrays Misses' costume
No. 4664 (copyright), again illustrated
on page 85. The pattern is in 7 sizes
for misses from 10 to 16 years of age,
and costs 1s. 6d. or 35 cents. To make
the costume for a miss of 12 years,
needs 6¾ yards of goods 22 inches wide.

FIGURE NO. 367 A.—LADIES' ULSTER. — This represents
Ladies' ulster No. 4727 (copyright), again illustrated on page
87 of this publication. The pattern is in 13 sizes for ladies
from 28 to 46 inches, bust measure, and costs 1s. 8d. or 40
cents. To make the garment for a lady of medium size, will
need 8⅝ yards of goods 22 inches wide, or 4⅞ yards 44 inches
wide, each with ⅞ yard of silk 20 inches wide to line the hood.

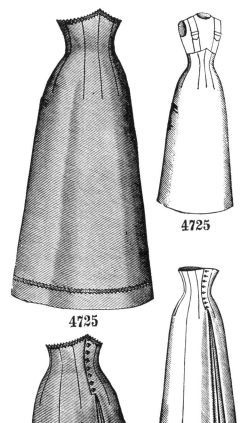

4725

FIGURE NO. 372 A.—MISSES' COAT.—
This illustrates Misses' coat No. 4699 (copyright), which is shown again on this page.
The pattern is in 9 sizes for misses from 8
to 16 years of age, and costs 1s. 3d. or 30
cents. To make the garment for a miss
of 12 years, will require 4¾ yards of
material 22 inches wide, or 2½ yards 44
inches wide, or 2 yards 54 inches wide.

NO. 4725.—MISSES' CORSELET PRINCESS
SKIRT, WITH SUSPENDERS (Copyright).—This
skirt forms part of the stylish toilette shown
at figure No. 382 A on page 89, where it is
portrayed developed in cheviot and trimmed
with passementerie. The pattern is in 7
sizes for misses from 10 to 16 years of age.
To make the skirt for a miss of 12 years, will
require 3¾ yards of material 22 inches
wide, or 2⅞ yards 30 inches wide, or 2¼
yards 44 inches wide. If goods 50 inches wide be chosen, 1⅞ yard will suffice.
Price of pattern, 1s. 3d. or 30 cents.

FIGURE NO. 350 A.—LADIES' STREET TOILETTE.—This consists of
Ladies' skirt No. 4700 (copyright), which is shown again on page 92;
and basque No. 4702 (copyright), seen on page 89. The skirt pattern
is in 9 sizes for ladies from 20 to 36 inches, waist measure, and costs
1s. 6d. or 35 cents. The basque pattern is in 13 sizes for ladies
from 28 to 46 inches, bust measure, and costs 1s. 3d. or 30 cents. For
a lady of medium size, they need 11⅜ yards of goods 22 inches wide.

4682

4682

NO. 4682.—
MISSES' JACK-
ET (Copyright).
—This pattern
is again shown
at figures Nos.
3 8 1 A and
373 A on pages
8 4 and 8 6.
The jacket is
here illustrat-
ed made of
cloth, and ma-
chine-stitch-
ing and but-
tons form a
neat finish.
The pattern is
in 9 sizes for
misses from 8
to 16 years of
age. To make
the jacket for a miss of 12 years, will require 4⅛ yards of material 22
inches wide, or 2 yards 44 inches wide. If goods 54 inches wide be
selected, then 1⅝ yard will suffice. Price of pattern, 1s. or 25 cents.

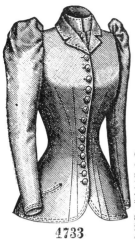

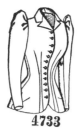

4733

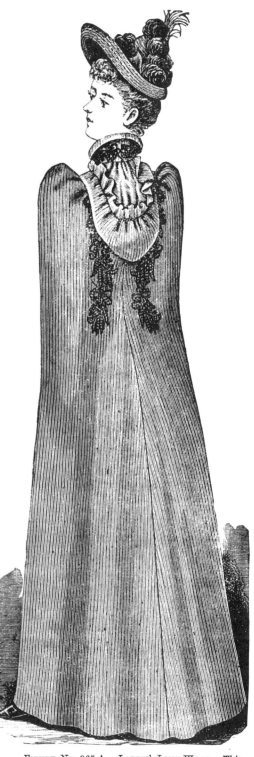

No. 4733.—LADIES' BASQUE
(Copyright). — Another view
of this basque may be ob-
served by referring to figure
No. 338 A on page 89 of this
publication. The basque may
be worn with any style of
skirt, and without the standing collar and chemisette, as
shown in the small engraving.
The pattern is in 13 sizes for
ladies from 28 to 46 inches, bust measure. To make the basque for a lady of medium
size, requires 3¾ yards of goods 22 inches wide, or 1⅞ yard 44 inches wide. If material 50 inches wide be selected, 1¾ yard will suffice. Price of pattern, 1s. 3d. or 30 cts.

4689

No. 4689.—LA-
DIES' RUSSIAN
BLOUSE (WITH
FITTED BODY-LIN-
ING, WHICH MAY
BE OMITTED)
(Copyright).—
Other views of
this blouse may
be observed at fig-
ures Nos. 340 A
and 349 A on
pages 88 and 93.
India or China
silk, cashmere,
serge or vicuna
will develop prettily by the mode. The pattern is in 13 sizes for ladies from 28 to 46 inches,
bust measure. For a lady of medium size, it requires 6⅜ yards of goods 22 inches wide, or
3¼ yards 44 inches wide, or 3 yards 50 inches wide. Price of pattern, 1s. 3d. or 30 cents.

4692

No. 4692.—LITTLE GIRLS' COAT
(Copyright).—At figure No. 393 A
on page 94 this little coat is represented differently made up. It
is here pictured developed in plain
cloth, with ribbon and buttons for
decoration. The pattern is in 6
sizes for little girls from 2 to 7
years old. For a girl of 5 years,
it needs 6¼ yards of goods 22
inches wide, or 2⅓ yards 44
inches wide, or 2⅝ yards 54 inches
wide. Price of pattern, 10d. or 20 cts.

FIGURE No. 365 A.—LADIES' LONG WRAP.—This
portrays Ladies' long wrap No. 4666 (copyright),
three views of which may be observed by referring
to page 90 of this publication. The pattern is in 10
sizes for ladies from 28 to 46 inches, bust measure,
and costs 1s. 8d. or 40 cents. To make the wrap
of one material for a lady of medium size, requires
4 yards 44 inches wide, or 3⅜ yards 54 inches
wide. In the combination pictured on page 90, it
needs 3⅜ yards of fancy cloaking 54 inches wide,
together with 1⅛ yard of silk 20 inches wide.

FIGURE No. 344 A. — LADIES' COSTUME.—This portrays Ladies' costume No. 4730 (copyright), again shown on page 86. A full front view of the costume is given at figure No. 342 A on page 87. The pattern is in 13 sizes for ladies from 28 to 46 inches, bust measure, and costs 1s. 8d. or 40 cents. For a lady of medium size, the costume will require 9¼ yards of material 22 inches wide, or 4⅞ yards 44 inches wide. Of goods 50 inches wide, 4½ yards will be sufficient.

FIGURE No. 345 A.—LADIES' COSTUME.—This is Ladies' costume No. 4723 (copyright), again shown on page 86. A full front view is given at figure No. 343 A on page 87. The pattern is in 13 sizes for ladies from 28 to 46 inches, bust measure, and costs 1s. 8d. or 40 cents. For a lady of medium size, it needs 11¾ yards of goods 22 inches wide.

4691

4691

4691

FIGURE No. 356 A.—LADIES' COSTUME.—This is Ladies' costume No. 4669 (copyright), again shown on page 87. The pattern is in 13 sizes for ladies from 28 to 46 inches, bust measure, and costs 1s. 8d. or 40 cents. For a lady of medium size, it requires 8 yards of material 22 inches wide, or 4¼ yards 44 inches wide, or 4 yards 50 inches wide.

No. 4691.—MISSES' JOSEPHINE OR EMPIRE DRESS (Copyright).—At figure No. 377 A on page 90 this quaint dress is again pictured. The garment is here shown developed in white woollen delaine, and white ribbon trims it. It may be made high or low in the neck and with long or short sleeves. The pattern is in 9 sizes for misses from 8 to 16 years of age. To make the dress for a miss of 12 years, requires 7⅛ yards of material 22 inches wide, or 5⅜ yards 30 inches wide, or 3⅞ yards 44 inches wide. Price of pattern, 1s. 3d. or 30 cents.

FIGURE NO. 355 A.—LADIES' RUSSIAN COAT.—
This illustrates Ladies' Russian coat No. 4665
(copyright), which is again pictured on page 91
of this publication. The pattern is in 13 sizes for
ladies from 28 to 46 inches, bust measure, and
costs 1s. 6d. or 35 cents. To make the coat of
one material for a lady of medium size, requires
6¼ yards 22 inches wide, or 3⅝ yards 44 inches
wide, or 2⅞ yards 54 inches wide. In the combination shown on page 91, it needs 2¾ yards of
cheviot 54 inches wide, with 1⅝ yard of silk.

**FIGURE NO. 349 A.
—LADIES' RUSSIAN
BLOUSE.—**This illus-
trates Ladies' Rus-
sian blouse No. 4689
(copyright), again re-
presented on page 91.
India or China silk,
serge, vicuna, vi-
gogne, cashmere or
albatross cloth will
develop attractively
by the mode. The
pattern is in 13 sizes
for ladies from 28 to
46 inches, bust meas-
ure, and costs 1s.
3d. or 30 cents. For
a lady of medium size,
it requires 6⅜ yards
of material 22 inches
wide, or 3¼ yards
44 inches wide, or 3
yards 50 inches wide.

**FIGURE NO. 394 A.—CHILD'S
DRESS.** — This illustrates
Child's dress No. 4671 (copyright), which is shown again
on page 86 of this publication.
The pattern is in 7 sizes for
children from ½ to 6 years
old, and costs 10d. or 20
cents. For a child of 5 years,
the dress needs 3¾ yards of
goods 22 inches wide, or 3
yards 27 inches wide, or 2¼
yards 36 inches wide.

**FIGURE NO. 339 A.—LADIES' VISITING TOILETTE.—This consists of Ladies' Wat-
teau coat No. 4679 (copyright), and bell skirt No. 4728 (copyright), both of which
are shown again on page 88 of this publication. In the present instance the coat
is pictured made of castor cloth, with a braid ornament for trimming. The skirt is
of herring-bone cheviot. The coat pattern is in 13 sizes for ladies from 28 to
46 inches, bust measure; the skirt pattern is in 9 sizes for ladies from 20 to
36 inches, waist measure; and each costs 1s. 6d. or 35 cents. To make the
toilette for a lady of medium size, needs 7¼ yards of goods 44 inches wide.

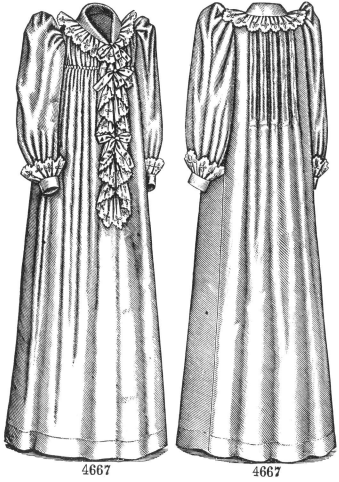

4667   **4667**

No. 4667. — LADIES' NIGHT-GOWN (Copyright). — Cambric was used in making this night-gown, and ruffles of embroidery and ribbon bows trim it. India silk, wash silk, Surah, lawn, cambric and nainsook are generally used for garments of this kind, and Italian or torchon lace, embroidery, feather-stitched bands, etc., are applied for decoration. The pattern is in 10 sizes for ladies from 28 to 46 inches, bust measure. To make the garment for a lady of medium size, will require $10\frac{3}{8}$ yards of material 22 inches wide, or $5\frac{3}{4}$ yards 36 inches wide. Price of pattern, 1s. 6d. or 35 cents.

4697   **4697**   **4697**

No. 4697. — MISSES' BELL SKIRT, SEWED TO A GIRDLE HAVING SUSPENDERS (Copyright). — This stylish skirt is again illustrated at figure No. 378 A on page 87. The pattern is in 7 sizes for misses from 10 to 16 years of age. To make the garment for a miss of 12 years, will require $3\frac{3}{8}$ yards of material 22 inches wide, or $2\frac{5}{8}$ yards 30 inches wide, or $1\frac{5}{8}$ yard 44 inches wide, or $1\frac{1}{2}$ yard 50 inches wide. Price of pattern, 1s. 3d. or 30 cents.

FIGURE NO. 362 A. — LADIES' OUTDOOR TOILETTE. — This consists of Ladies' skirt No. 4650 (copyright), shown again on page 81; and wrap No. 4703 (copyright), on page 89. The skirt pattern is in 9 sizes for ladies from 20 to 36 inches, waist measure, and costs 1s. 6d. or 35 cents. The wrap pattern is in 10 sizes for ladies from 28 to 46 inches, bust measure, and costs 1s. 3d. or 30 cents. For a lady of medium size, the skirt needs $6\frac{3}{8}$ yds. of goods 22 ins. wide, and the wrap $4\frac{3}{4}$ yards in the same width.

4694

4694

4694

4694

4694

No. 4694.—Ladies' Bell Skirt, with Slight Train (Perforated for Round Length, and Sewed to a Girdle Having Suspenders) (Copyright).—This skirt is also portrayed at figure No. 357 A on page 86. The material here pictured is Russian-blue serge, and gimp supplies the trimming. The pattern provides for two styles of girdles that may be worn with or without suspenders. All sorts of seasonable woollens are adapted to the mode, and braid, gimp, galloon, passementerie, ribbon, fancy bands and machine or fancy stitching will be appropriate garniture. The pattern is in 9 sizes for ladies from 20 to 36 inches, waist measure. To make the skirt for a lady of medium size, will require $5\frac{5}{8}$ yards of goods 22 inches wide, or 4 yards 30 inches wide, or $3\frac{1}{8}$ yards 44 inches wide, or $2\frac{3}{4}$ yards 50 inches wide. Price of pattern, 1s. 6d. or 35 cents.

Figure No. 352 A.—Ladies' Visiting Toilette.—This consists of Ladies' coat No. 4670 (copyright), shown again on this page; and skirt No. 4728 (copyr't), on page 88. The coat pattern is in 13 sizes for ladies from 28 to 46 inches, bust measure, and costs 1s. 6d. or 35 cents. The skirt pattern is in 9 sizes for ladies from 20 to 36 inches, waist measure, and costs 1s. 6d. or 35 cents. For a lady of medium size, the coat needs $8\frac{1}{2}$ yards of goods 22 inches wide, and the skirt $6\frac{1}{8}$ yards in the same width.

4720

4720

4720

No. 4720.—Misses' Long Basque (Known as the Norfolk Jacket) (Copyright).—This pattern, also illustrated at figure No. 375 A on page 84, is in 7 sizes for misses from 10 to 16 years of age. For a miss of 12 years, it needs $4\frac{1}{2}$ yards of goods 22 inches wide, or $2\frac{1}{4}$ yards 44 inches wide, or $1\frac{7}{8}$ yard 54 inches wide. Price of pattern. 1s. or 25 cts.

4670

4670

4670

No. 4729.—Girls' Costume, with Eton Jacket (Copyright). —This jaunty costume may be prettily developed in crépon. cashmere, camel's-hair, piqué or percale, and plain or fancy braids, gimp or galloon will trim it handsomely. The pattern is in 8 sizes for girls from 5 to 12 years of age. To make the costume for a girl of 8 years, will require 5¼ yards of goods 22 inches wide, or 4 yards 30 inches wide. Of material 44 inches wide, 2⅝ yards will suffice. Price of pattern, 1s. or 25 cents.

4729

4729

No. 4670.—Ladies' Watteau Coat (Copyright).—At figure No. 352 A on this page, this stylish coat is pictured made of tan cloth, with braid ornaments for decoration. It will also develop prettily in faced cloth, serge, camel's-hair, Bengaline, armure and various other materials of silken or woollen texture. The pattern is in 13 sizes for ladies from 28 to 46 inches, bust measure. To make the garment for a lady of medium size, will require 8½ yards of material 22 inches wide, or 4⅞ yards 44 inches wide. If goods 54 inches wide be selected, then 3¾ yards will prove sufficient. Price of pattern, 1s. 6d. or 35 cents.

4700

4700

4700

No. 4700. — Ladies' Skirt, with Four Gores Having Bias Edges, and Slight Train (Perforated for Round Length) (Copyright). —Different illustrations of this skirt are given at figures Nos. 351 A and 350 A on pages 88 and 91 of this publication. The skirt is here represented made of striped wool goods. The novel effect of the bias edges is brought out to best advantage in striped goods, but checks, plaids and plain textures are also nicely adapted to the mode. The pattern is in 9 sizes for ladies from 20 to 36 inches, waist measure. To make the skirt for a lady of medium size, will require 6¾ yards of material 22 inches wide, or 3¾ yards 44 inches wide. If 50-inch-wide goods be chosen, then 3½ yards will prove amply sufficient. Price of pattern, 1s. 6d. or 35 cents.

Figure No. 397 A.—Little Boys' Blouse Costume.—This depicts Little Boys' blouse costume No. 4715, shown on page 84. The pattern is in 6 sizes for little boys from 2 to 7 years of age, and costs 1s. or 25 cents. Of one material for a boy of 5 years, the costume requires 4⅝ yards 27 inches wide, or 2⅜ yards 54 inches wide. In the combination shown on page 84, it needs 3¾ yards of striped and 1 yard of plain flannel 27 inches wide.

FIGURE No. 396 A.—LITTLE BOYS' SUIT.—This consists of Little Boys' Russian suit No. 4717, which is again shown on page 88; and cap No. 3167 (copyright), seen on page 66. The suit pattern is in 6 sizes for little boys from 2 to 7 years of age, and costs 1s. or 25 cents. The cap pattern is in 6 sizes from 6¼ to 7½, hat sizes, and costs 5d. or 10 cts. For goods needed, see pages 66 and 88.

4709

No. 4709. — BOYS' BOX OVERCOAT. — The accompanying engravings picture an overcoat stylishly developed in melton, with machine-stitching for a completion. The pattern is in 10 sizes for boys from 7 to 16 years of age. To make the overcoat for a boy of 11 years, will require 3⅜ yards of material 27 inches wide, or 1⅝ yard of goods 54 inches wide. Price of pattern, 1s. 3d. or 30 cents.

4709

4695

No. 4695.— LADIES' COAT (WITH BODY LINING) (Copyright).—By referring to figure No. 370 A on page 85 of this issue, another view of this coat may be observed. The pattern is in 13 sizes for ladies from 28 to 46 inches, bust meas. To make the garment for a lady of medium size, will require 6¾ yards of material 22 inches wide, or 4¾ yards 44 inches wide. If goods 54 inches wide be selected, then 3⅝ yards will prove sufficient. Price of pattern, 1s. 6d. or 35 cents.

4695

4665

4665

No. 4665.—LADIES' RUSSIAN COAT (Copyright).—Other views of this garment are given at figures Nos. 354 A and 355 A on pages 88 and 92. The pattern is in 13 sizes for ladies from 28 to 46 inches, bust

4665

measure. For a lady of medium size, the coat needs 2¾ yards of cheviot 54 inches wide, with 1⅝ yard of silk. Of one material, it requires 6¼ yards 22 inches wide, or 3⅝ yards 44 inches wide, or 2⅞ yards 54 inches wide. Price of pattern, 1s. 6d. or 35 cents.

FIGURE No. 383 A.—MISSES' ULSTER.—This illustrates Misses' ulster No. 4726 (copyright), again shown on page 94. The pattern is in 9 sizes for misses from 8 to 16 years of age, and costs 1s. 6d. or 35 cents. For a miss of 12 years, it will require 5¾ yards of goods 22 inches wide, or 3⅛ yards 44 inches wide, each with ⅞ yard of silk 20 inches wide to line the hood.

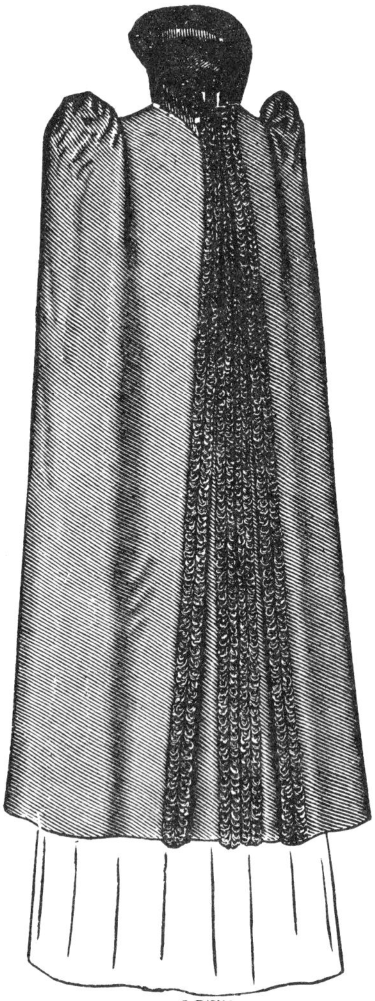

4675

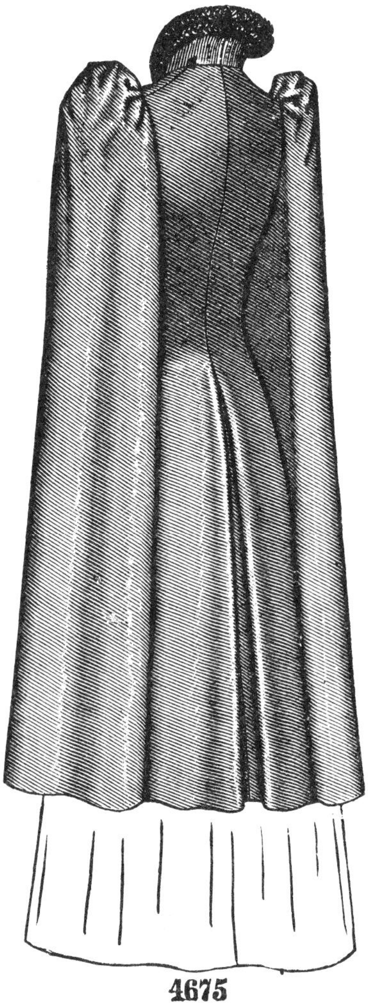

4675

No. 4675.—Ladies' Cape, with Russian Fronts (In Three-Quarter Length) (Copyright).—This stylish cape is again illustrated at figure No. 364 A on page 90 of this publication. The pattern is in 10 sizes for ladies from 28 to 46 inches, bust measure. To make the cape for a lady of medium size, will require $3\frac{3}{8}$ yards of material 44 inches wide, or $2\frac{5}{8}$ yards 54 inches wide. Price of pattern, 1s. 6d. or 35 cents.

Figure No. 392 A.—Little Girls' Russian Cloak.—This depicts Little Girls' Russian cloak No. 4688 (copyright), shown again on page 84. The pattern is in 9 sizes for little girls from 1 to 9 years old, and costs 10d. or 20 cents. For a girl of 5 years, it needs 5 yards of goods 22 inches wide, or $2\frac{5}{8}$ yards 44 inches wide, or $2\frac{3}{8}$ yards 54 inches wide.

Figure No. 393 A.—Little Girls' Coat.—This illustrates Little Girls' coat No. 4692 (copyright), pictured on page 92. The pattern is in 6 sizes for little girls from 2 to 7 years of age, and costs 10d. or 20 cents. For a girl of 5 years, the coat needs $6\frac{1}{4}$ yards of goods 22 inches wide, or $2\frac{7}{8}$ yards 44 inches wide, or $2\frac{5}{8}$ yards 54 inches wide.

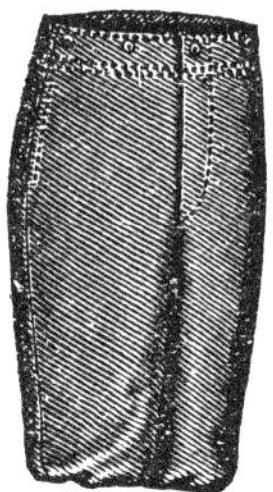

4705

No. 4705.—Boys' Knickerbocker Trousers, with a Fly.—Flannel was employed for the construction of the trousers here pictured, and machine-stitching forms a neat completion. The pattern is in 14 sizes for boys from 3 to 16 years of age. To make the garment for a boy of 11 years, will require $1\frac{5}{8}$ yard of material 27 inches wide, or $\frac{7}{8}$ yard 54 inches wide. Price of pattern, 7d. or 15 cents.

4705

4663

4663

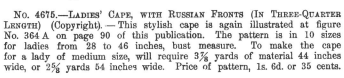

4663

No. 4663.—Girls' Dress (Copyr't).—Another view of this stylish little dress is given at figure No. 380 A on page 84 of this issue. A dainty combination of dark cashmere and plain silk is here pictured in the dress, and gilt gimp and buttons trim it. The pattern is in 8 sizes for girls from 5 to 12 years of age. For a girl of 8 years, it needs $3\frac{3}{8}$ yards of dress goods 40 inches wide, with $\frac{7}{8}$ yard of silk. Of one material, it calls for $5\frac{5}{8}$ yards 22 inches wide, or $2\frac{3}{4}$ yards 44 inches wide. Price of pattern, 1s. or 25 cents.

4681

4681

No. 4681.—Little Girls' Cloak (Copyright).—At figure No. 390 A on page 88 this cloak is again shown. It is here pictured made of plain cloth, with machine-stitching for a finish. A similar garment will develop stylishly in Bengaline, faille, brocaded silk or any seasonable wool goods. The loose edges of the capes may be pinked. The pattern is in 6 sizes for little girls from 1 to 6 years old. For a girl of 5 years, it needs $5\frac{7}{8}$ yards of goods 22 inches wide, or $3\frac{1}{4}$ yards 44 inches wide, or $2\frac{5}{8}$ yards 54 inches wide. Price of pattern, 10d. or 20 cents.

4681

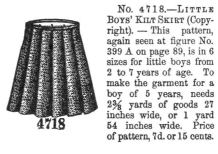

No. 4718.—LITTLE
BOYS' KILT SKIRT (Copy-
right). — This pattern,
again seen at figure No.
399 A on page 89, is in 6
sizes for little boys from
2 to 7 years of age. To
make the garment for a
boy of 5 years, needs
2⅜ yards of goods 27
inches wide, or 1 yard
54 inches wide. Price
of pattern, 7d. or 15 cents.

4718

FIGURE NO. 360 A.—LADIES' OUTDOOR TOILETTE.—This
consists of Ladies' belt No. 4693 (copyright), shown on page
86; Eton jacket No. 4735 (copyright), on page 84; and
blouse No. 3802 (copyright), on page 12. The belt pattern
is in 9 sizes for ladies from 20 to 36 inches, waist measure,
and costs 5d. or 10 cents. The jacket and blouse patterns
are each in 13 sizes for ladies from 28 to 46 inches, bust
measure: the jacket costing 10d. or 20 cents; and the blouse,
1s. 3d. or 30 cents. For goods needed, see pages 12, 84 and 86.

FIGURE NO. 395 A.— LITTLE
BOYS' FAUNTLEROY SUIT.—This
consists of Little Boys' Fauntleroy
costume No. 4716, shown on page
84; and cap No. 3166 (copyright),
on page 14. The costume pattern is in 6 sizes for little boys
from 2 to 7 years old, and
costs 1s. or 25 cents. The cap
pattern is in 6 sizes from 6¼
to 7½, hat sizes, and costs 5d
or 10 cents. For materials
needed, see pages 14 and 84.

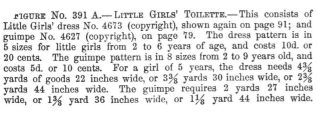

FIGURE NO. 391 A.— LITTLE GIRLS' TOILETTE.—This consists of
Little Girls' dress No. 4673 (copyright), shown again on page 91; and
guimpe No. 4627 (copyright), on page 79. The dress pattern is in
5 sizes for little girls from 2 to 6 years of age, and costs 10d. or
20 cents. The guimpe pattern is in 8 sizes from 2 to 9 years old, and
costs 5d. or 10 cents. For a girl of 5 years, the dress needs 4⅜
yards of goods 22 inches wide, or 3¾ yards 30 inches wide, or 2⅜
yards 44 inches wide. The guimpe requires 2 yards 27 inches
wide, or 1⅜ yard 36 inches wide, or 1⅛ yard 44 inches wide.

FIGURE NO. 341 A.—LADIES' RUSSIAN TOILETTE.—This consists of Ladies' Russian blouse No. 4672 (copyright), seen
on page 89; and bell skirt No. 4482 (copyright), on page 35.
For sizes, prices and goods needed, see pages 35 and 89.

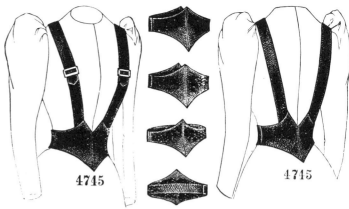

No. 4745.—Ladies' Girdles (Copyright).—At figure No. 421 A on page 100 one of these girdles is again portrayed. The pattern is in 9 sizes for ladies from 20 to 36 inches, waist measure. For a lady of medium size, the girdle with suspenders will require ¾ yard of material 20 inches wide, or ¾ yard of goods 44 inches wide. The girdle without suspenders needs ½ yard of goods 20 inches wide, or ½ yard 44 inches wide. Price of pattern, 7d. or 15 cents.

FIGURE NO. 348 A. —LADIES' R U S S I A N BLOUSE.—This represents Ladies' Russian blouse No. 4672 (copyright), also pictured on page 89. Gray cloth, and myrtle-green velvet overlaid with Russian embroidery were here used for the blouse. The pattern is in 13 sizes for ladies from 28 to 46 inches, bust measure, and costs 1s. 3d. or 30 cents. For a lady of medium size, it requires 5½ yards of goods 22 inches wide, or 3 yards 44 inches wide, or 2¾ yards 50 inches wide.

No. 4789.—MISSES' DRESS, WITH FITTED LININGS (Copyright).—This pattern is in 7 sizes for misses from 10 to 16 years of age. For a miss of 12 years, it requires 2⅛ yards of plain dress goods 40 inches wide, with 2⅞ yards of polka-dotted silk. Of one material, it needs 6½ yards 22 ins wide, or 3⅛ yards 44 ins. wide. Price of pattern, 1s. 3d. or 30 cts.

FIGURE NO. 407 A.—LADIES' PROMENADE TOILETTE.—This consists of Ladies' wrap No. 4741 (copyright), shown on page 102; and skirt No. 4631 (copyright), on page 83. The wrap pattern is in 10 sizes for ladies from 28 to 46 inches, bust measure, and costs 1s. 6d. or 35 cents. The skirt pattern is in 9 sizes for ladies from 20 to 36 inches, waist measure, and costs 1s. 6d. or 35 cents. For goods needed, see pages 83 and 102.

No. 4750.—MISSES' AND GIRLS' D R E S S SLEEVE (WITH FITTED LINING) (Copyright).— This sleeve is appropriate for any style of dress body, and may be made with or without the cuff. All sorts of dress fabrics will develop well by the mode. The pattern is in 8 sizes from 2 to 16 years of age. To make a pair of sleeves for a miss of 12 years, will require 1⅜ yard of material 22 inches wide, or 1¼ yard 30 ins. wide, or ¾ yard either 44 or 50 inches wide. Price of pattern, 5d. or 10 cents.

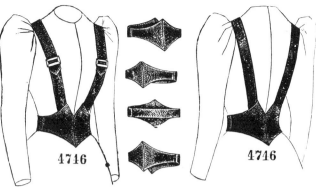

4716 **4716**

No. 4846.—Child's Bon-
net (Copyr't).—This pattern
is in 8 sizes for children
from ½ to 7 years of age.
For a child of 5 years, the
bonnet calls for ⅜ yard of
goods 20 inches or more
wide, with ⅝ yard of silk
20 inches wide. Of one
material, it needs ⅝ yard
20 inches or more wide.
Price of pattern, 5d. or 10 cts.

4846

No. 4746.—Misses' and Girls' Girdles (Copyright).—These girdles
are shown developed in velvet. The pattern is in 6 sizes from 6 to
16 years of age. To make the girdle with suspenders for a miss of 12
years, will require ⅝ yard of goods 20 inches or more in width. The
girdle without suspenders will call for ½ yard of material 20
inches or more in width. Price of pattern, 5d. or 10 cents.

4722 **4722**

No. 4722.—Ladies' Petticoat (Fitted to Fasten Low on the Corset) (Copyright).—This petticoat, which is especially desirable for stout women, is pictured
developed in silk, and a pinked ruffle of the material is at the lower edge. The
pattern is in 9 sizes for ladies from 20 to 36 inches, waist measure. To make the
garment for a lady of medium size, requires 5⅞ yards of material 20 inches wide, or
4⅜ yards 27 inches wide, or 3½ yards 36 inches wide. Price of pattern, 1s. or 25 cts.

No. 4749.—Child's Dress
(Also Known as the
Gretchen Dress) (Copy-
right). — This picturesque
little gown is again shown
at figure No. 453 A on page
101. It is here pictured
made of white cambric and
trimmed with embroidered
insertion and edging. The
pattern is in 7 sizes for
children from ½ to 6 years
old. For a child of 5 years,
it requires 4 yards of material 22 inches wide, or 3½
yards 27 inches wide, or
2½ yards 36 inches wide.
or 2 yards 44 inches wide.
Price of pattern, 10d. or 20 cts.

4749 **4749**

Figure No. 415 A.—Ladies' Russian Toilette.—This consists of
Ladies' basque No. 4785 (copyr't). shown on page 100; and cornet skirt
No. 4631 (copyr't), on page 83. The basque pattern is in 13 sizes for
ladies from 28 to 46 ins., bust meas., and costs 1s. 3d. or 30 cents. The
skirt pattern is in 9 sizes for ladies from 20 to 36 ins., waist meas., and
costs 1s. 6d. or 35 cents. For goods needed. see pages 83 and 100.

4767

4767

No. 4 7 6 7.—
Misses' Coat
(Suitable for
Seal-Skin,
Plush, etc.)
(Copyright).—
A different illus-
tration of this
coat is given
at figure No.
403 A on page
96. The pattern

4767

is in 7 sizes for misses from 10 to 16 years old.
3⅞ yards of material 22 inches wide, or 1⅞ yard 44 inches wide, or 1¾ yard
50 inches wide, or 1⅝ yard 54 inches wide.

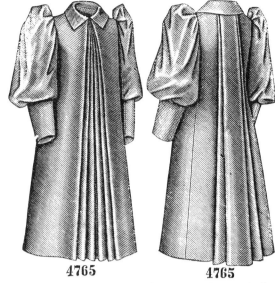

4765   **4765**

No. 4765.—Girls' Watteau Coat (Copyright).—This coat is also
represented at figure No. 443 A on page 99. The pattern is in 10
sizes for girls from 3 to 12 years of age. For a girl of 8 years, it
needs 6 yards of goods 22 inches wide, or 3⅜ yards 44 inches
wide, or 3 yards 54 inches wide. Price of pattern, 1s. 3d. or 30 cts.

For a miss of 12 years, it calls for
Price of pattern, 1s. 3d. or 30 cents.

4707   **4707**

No. 4707.—Little Boys' Overcoat
(Known as the Covert Coat) (To be
Worn with Kilts and Short Trousers).—Another representation of this
comfortable little garment is depicted
at figure No. 399 A on page 89. The
pattern is in 6 sizes for little boys
from 2 to 7 years old. For a boy of
5 years, it needs 2¼ yards of goods
27 inches wide, or 1⅛ yard 54 inches
wide. Price of pattern, 10d. or 20 cts.

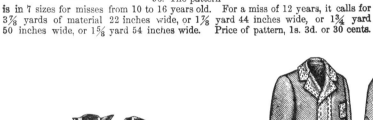

4762   **4762**

Figure No. 446 A.—Girls' Eton Costume.—This illustrates Girls' costume No.
4762 (copyright), shown again on this page.
The pattern is in 10 sizes for girls from 3
to 12 years of age, and costs 1s. 3d. or 30
cents. To make the costume of one material for a girl of 8 years, requires 5⅞
yards 22 inches wide, or 3 yards 44 inches wide, or 2⅝ yards 50 inches wide.

No. 4762.—Girls' Eton Costume (Copyright).
—This pattern, also shown at figure No. 446 A
on this page, is in 10 sizes for girls from 3 to
12 years of age. To make the costume for a girl
of 8 years, will require 2¾ yards of serge 40 inches wide, with 1 yard of silk 20 inches wide. Of
one material, it needs 5⅞ yards 22 inches wide,
or 3 yards 44 inches wide, or 2⅝ yards 50 inches wide. Price of pattern, 1s. 3d. or 30 cents.

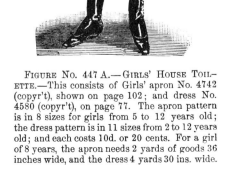

Figure No. 447 A.—Girls' House Toilette.—This consists of Girls' apron No. 4742
(copyr't), shown on page 102; and dress No.
4580 (copyr't), on page 77. The apron pattern
is in 8 sizes for girls from 5 to 12 years
old; the dress pattern is in 11 sizes from 2 to 12 years
old; and each costs 10d. or 20 cents. For a girl
of 8 years, the apron needs 2 yards of goods 36
inches wide, and the dress 4 yards 30 ins. wide.

4784   **4784**

No. 4784.—LITTLE GIRLS' CLOAK, WITH WAT-
TEAU BACK (Copyright).—At figure No. 450 A on
page 98, this cloak may be again observed. The
pattern is in 7 sizes for little girls from ½ to 6 years
of age. For a girl of 5 years, it requires 4¾ yards
of goods 22 inches wide, or 2½ yards 44 inches
wide, or 2¼ yards 54 inches wide. As pictured,
it needs 2¼ yards of cloth 54 inches wide, with ½
yard of velvet. Price of pattern, 10d. or 20 cents.

FIGURE No. 439 A.—MISSES'
MARGUERITE BASQUE.—This portrays Misses' basque No. 4753
(copyright), again shown on page
98. The pattern is in 9 sizes for misses
from 8 to 16 years of age, and costs 1s.
or 25 cents. To make the basque for a
miss of 12 years, will require 3 yards of
material 22 inches wide, or 1½ yard 44
inches wide. In the combination pictured
on page 98, it calls for 1¼ yard of dress
goods 40 inches wide, with 1¼ yard of silk.

FIGURE No. 440 A. — MISSES' MARGUERITE
BASQUE.—This depicts Misses' basque No. 4796
(copyright), which is again illustrated on page 98.
India silk, and velvet overlaid with lace are here
united in the basque, and ribbon bows trim it
effectively. The pattern is in 7 sizes for misses
from 10 to 16 years of age, and costs 1s. or 25
cents. To make the basque for a miss of 12
years, will require 4 yards of material 22 inches
wide, or 2 yards 44 inches wide, or 1⅝ yard
50 inches wide. In the combination illustrated on
page 98, it calls for ⅞ yard of dress goods 40
inches wide, with 3⅜ yards of silk 20 inches wide.

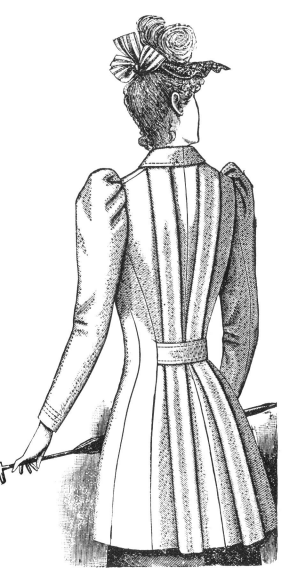

FIGURE No. 369 A.—LADIES' RUSSIAN REEFER JACKET.
—This represents Ladies' Russian reefer jacket No. 4732
(copyright), which is again portrayed on page 91. The
pattern is in 13 sizes for ladies from 28 to 46 inches, bust
measure, and costs 1s. 3d. or 30 cents. For a lady of
medium size, it needs 5¼ yards of goods 22 inches wide,
or 2⅝ yards 44 inches wide, or 2¼ yards 54 inches wide.

4726

No. 4726.—
MISSES' UL-
STER (TO BE
MADE WITH
OR WITHOUT A
HOOD) (Copy-
right).— At
figure No.
383 A on page
91 this stylish
and service-
able ulster
may be again
observed.
Mixed cheviot
was here used
in the con-
struction of
the garment,
and machine-
stitching, silk
and buttons furnish the decoration. For general uses it will
develop nicely in serge, tweed,
striped or checked cheviot or
heavy coatings. The pattern is
in 9 sizes for misses from 8 to
16 years old. For a miss of 12
years, it needs 5¾ yards of material 22 inches wide, or 3⅛
yards 44 inches wide, or 2⅜
yards 54 inches wide, each
with ⅞ yard of silk 20 inches
wide to line the hood. Price
of pattern, 1s. 6d. or 35 cents.

4726      **4726**

4738

No. 4738.—Ladies' Costume, with a Short Train (Perforated for Round Length) (Copyright).—This handsomely shaped costume is also shown at figure No. 410 A on page 98. Cheviot was the material chosen for its development in the present instance, and machine-stitching and buttons provide a stylish and appropriate completion. The pattern is in 13 sizes for ladies from 28 to 46 inches, bust measure. To make the costume for a lady of medium size, will require 12½ yards of material 22 inches wide, or 6⅜ yards 44 inches wide, or 5¾ yards 50 inches wide. Price of pattern, 1s. 8d. or 40 cents.

4772

No. 4772.—Ladies' Coat, with Vest (Copyright).—Hunter's-green cloth and heavy silk are combined in this coat, with fur bindings for trimming. The pattern is in 13 sizes for ladies from 28 to 46 inches, bust measure. For a lady of medium size, it needs 7⅝ yards of goods 22 inches wide, or 3¾ yards 44 inches wide, or 3⅛ yards 54 inches wide. In the combination shown, it needs 2¼ yards of cloth 54 inches wide, with 4 yards of silk. Price of pattern, 1s. 6d. or 35 cts.

Figure No. 402 A.—Misses' Long Wrap.—This illustrates Misses' wrap No. 4776 (copyright), which is also pictured on page 101. The pattern is in 7 sizes for misses from 10 to 16 years of age, and costs 1s. 6d. or 35 cents. For a miss of 12 years, it will require 9⅛ yards of material 22 inches wide, or 5 yards 44 inches wide, or 4⅛ yards 54 inches wide.

Figure No. 403 A.—Misses' Toilette.—This consists of Misses' coat No. 4767 (copyright), shown on page 97; and corselet Princess skirt No. 4725 (copyright), on page 91. Both patterns are in 7 sizes for misses from 10 to 16 years old, and each costs 1s. 3d. or 30 cts. Of goods 22 inches wide, for a miss of 12 years, the coat needs 3⅞ yards, and the skirt 3¾ yards.

No. 4737.—Ladies' Costume, with Demi-Train (Perforated for Round Length) (Copyright).—This modish costume is again shown at figure No. 409 A on page 98. An artistic combination of dress goods and silk was here effected, with ribbon and a ruffle of the material for garniture. The pattern is in 13 sizes for ladies from 28 to 46 inches, bust measure. For a lady of medium size, it will require 5½ yards of dress goods 40 inches wide, with 2½ yards of silk 20 inches wide. Of one material, it calls for 11½ yards 22 inches wide, or 5¾ yards 44 inches wide, or 5 yards 50 inches wide. Price of pattern, 1s. 8d. or 40 cents.

No. 4769.—Misses' Cape, with Watteau Back (Copyright).—This pattern, seen at figure No. 441 A on this page, is in 4 sizes for misses from 10 to 16 years of age. To make the garment for a miss of 12 years, will require 4¼ yards of material 22 inches wide, or 2¼ yards 44 inches wide. Of goods 54 inches wide, 1¾ yard will suffice. Price of pattern, 1s. or 25 cents.

Figure No. 441 A.—Ladies' Russian Costume.—This represents Ladies' Russian costume No. 4743 (copyright), also pictured on page 102. The pattern is in 13 sizes for ladies from 28 to 46 inches, bust measure, and costs 1s. 8d. or 40 cents. Of one material for a lady of medium size, it calls for 12⅛ yards 22 inches wide, or 6¼ yards 44 inches wide, or 5⅛ yards 50 inches wide.

No. 4795.—LADIES' BASQUE (KNOWN AS THE MARGUERITE BASQUE) (Copyright).—This basque is again shown at figures Nos. 405 A on page 100 and 406 A on page 102. The pattern is in 13 sizes for ladies from 28 to 46 inches, bust measure. To make the basque for a lady of medium size, requires 1 yard of dress goods 40 inches wide, with $3\frac{1}{2}$ yards of silk 20 inches wide. Of one material, it needs $4\frac{3}{8}$ yards 22 inches wide, or $2\frac{3}{8}$ yards 44 inches wide, or 2 yards 50 inches wide. Price of pattern, 1s. 3d. or 30 cts.

4795   4795

No. 4778.—GIRLS' DRESS (Copyright).— By referring to figure No. 449 A on page 98, another representation of this jaunty dress may be seen. China-blue serge was here used for the dress, and fancy gimp trims it effectively. The pattern is in 8 sizes for girls from 5 to 12 years of age. For a girl of 8 years, the dress requires $4\frac{3}{4}$ yards of material 22 inches wide, or $3\frac{5}{8}$ yards 30 inches wide. If goods 44 inches wide be chosen, then $2\frac{3}{8}$ yards will be sufficient. Price of pattern, 1s. or 25 cents.

4778

4778

4782

4782   4782

No. 4782.— MISSES' RIDING-HABIT BASQUE, WITH HIGH NECK AND STANDING COLLAR, OR OPEN NECK AND COAT COLLAR AND LAPELS (Copyright).—This pattern is in 7 sizes for misses from 10 to 16 years of age. For a miss of 12 years, it requires $2\frac{3}{8}$ yards of material 22 inches wide, or $1\frac{7}{8}$ yard 30 inches wide, or $1\frac{1}{4}$ yard 44 inches wide, or $1\frac{1}{8}$ yard 50 inches wide. Price of pattern, 1s. or 25 cents.

4781

4781   4781

No. 4781.— LADIES' RIDING-HABIT BASQUE, WITH HIGH NECK AND STANDING COLLAR, OR OPEN NECK AND COAT COLLAR AND LAPELS (Copyright).—This pattern is in 13 sizes for ladies from 28 to 46 inches, bust measure. Of one material for a lady of medium size, it requires $3\frac{1}{8}$ yards 22 inches wide, or $2\frac{1}{2}$ yards 30 inches wide, or $1\frac{5}{8}$ yard 44 inches wide, or $1\frac{3}{8}$ yard 50 inches wide. Price, 1s. 3d. or 30 cents.

FIGURE NO. 400 A.—MISSES' LONG COAT.—This portrays Misses' long coat No. 4775 (copyright), differently pictured on page 100 of this publication. The pattern is in 7 sizes for misses from 10 to 16 years of age, and costs 1s. 6d. or 35 cents. To make the garment for a miss of 12 years, will require $5\frac{7}{8}$ yards of material 22 inches wide, or $3\frac{1}{8}$ yards 44 inches wide, or $2\frac{1}{2}$ yards 54 inches wide.

FIGURE NO. 401 A.—MISSES' TOILETTE. —This consists of Misses' Watteau coat No. 4739 (copyright), depicted on page 100; and skirt No. 4236 (copyright), on page 54. Both patterns are in 7 sizes for misses from 10 to 16 years of age, and each costs 1s. 3d. or 30 cents. For a miss of 12 years, the toilette will require $4\frac{5}{8}$ yards of material 44 inches wide; the coat needing $2\frac{3}{4}$ yards, and the skirt, $1\frac{7}{8}$ yard.

4755   **4755**

NO. 4755.—LADIES' DRESS SLEEVE (TO BE MADE WITH A DEEP CUFF OR A GAUNTLET CUFF) (Copyright).—This pattern is in 7 sizes for ladies from 9 to 15 inches, arm measure, measuring about an inch below the bottom of the arm's-eye. For a lady whose arm measures 11 inches, a pair of sleeves with deep cuffs requires 1 yard of dress goods 40 inches wide, with ½ yard of velvet. Of one material, it requires ⅞ yard either 44 or 50 inches wide. A pair of sleeves with gauntlet cuffs calls for 2 yards 22 inches wide, or 1 yard 44 or 50 inches wide. Price, 5d. or 10 cts.

4751   **4751**

NO. 4751.—LADIES' DOUBLE-BREASTED VEST (Copyright).—This vest is again represented at figure No. 432 A on page 101. The pattern is in 13 sizes for ladies from 28 to 46 inches, bust measure. To make the vest for a lady of medium size, will require 1¾ yard of material 22 inches wide, or ⅞ yard 44 inches wide, or ¾ yard 54 inches wide. Price of pattern, 10d. or 20 cents.

4740

4740   **4740**

NO. 4740.—LADIES' BLOUSE OR SHIRT-WAIST (Copyright).—Striped washable silk is pictured in this blouse, with ruffles of the material for garniture. The pattern is in 13 sizes for ladies from 28 to 46 inches, bust measure. To make the garment for a lady of medium size, requires 4½ yards of material 22 inches wide, or 4⅛ yards 27 inches wide, or 3¼ yards 36 inches wide, or 2¼ yards 44 inches wide. Price of pattern, 1s. 3d. or 30 cents.

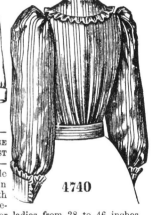

4793

4793   **4793**

NO. 4793.—MISSES' RUSSIAN BASQUE (Copyright).—This basque is given a different portrayal at figure No. 437 A on page 100. The pattern is in 7 sizes for misses from 10 to 16 years of age. To make the garment for a miss of 12 years, will call for 4⅝ yards of goods 22 inches wide, or 2¼ yards 44 inches wide, or 1⅞ yard 50 inches wide. Price of pattern, 1s. or 25 cents.

FIGURE No. 418 A.—LADIES' PRINCESS COSTUME.—This depicts Ladies' Princess costume No. 4779 (copyr't), shown again on this page. The pattern is in 13 sizes for ladies from 28 to 4⅜ inches, bust measure, and costs 1s. 8d. or 40 cents. For a lady of medium size, it needs 12⅜ yards of material 22 inches wide, or 6⅜ yards 44 inches wide, or 5½ yards 50 inches wide.

No. 4780.—LADIES' TEA-JACKET (Copyright).—At figure No. 425 A on page 102 this dainty-looking jacket is pictured worn with a bell skirt. Pale-blue cashmere was here used in developing the jacket, and ribbon and lace trim it prettily. The pattern is in 13 sizes for ladies from 28 to 46 inches, bust measure, and is adaptable to all soft materials of silken or woollen texture. To make the jacket for a lady of medium size, requires 5⅝ yards of goods 22 inches wide, or 3½ yards 36 inches wide, or 2⅞ yards 44 inches wide. Price of pattern, 1s. 3d. or 30 cents.

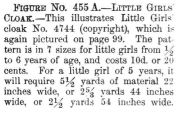

FIGURE NO. 455 A.—LITTLE GIRLS' CLOAK.—This illustrates Little Girls' cloak No. 4744 (copyright), which is again pictured on page 99. The pattern is in 7 sizes for little girls from ½ to 6 years of age, and costs 10d. or 20 cents. For a little girl of 5 years, it will require 5½ yards of material 22 inches wide, or 2⅝ yards 44 inches wide, or 2½ yards 54 inches wide.

FIGURE NO. 448 A.—GIRLS' DRESS. —This is Girls' dress No. 4777 (copyright), pictured on page 99. The pattern is in 8 sizes for girls from 5 to 12 years of age, and costs 1s. or 25 cents. Of one material for a girl of 8 years, it requires 5½ yards 22 inches wide, or 4¼ yards 30 inches wide, or 2⅝ yards 44 inches wide.

FIGURE NO. 441 A.—MISSES' CAPE.—This illustrates Misses' cape No. 4769 (copyright), shown again on this page. The pattern is in 4 sizes for misses from 10 to 16 years of age, and costs 1s. or 25 cents. For a miss of 12 years, it needs 4¼ yards of goods 22 inches wide, or 2⅛ yards 44 inches wide, or 1¾ yard 54 inches wide.

FIGURE NO. 442 A. — MISSES' RUSSIAN COAT.—This represents Misses' Russian coat No. 4754 (copyright), again depicted on page 99. Navy-blue serge and velvet are here combined in the jaunty coat, with stylish effect. The pattern is in 7 sizes for misses from 10 to 16 years of age, and costs 1s. 3d. or 30 cents. To make the coat for a miss of 12 years, will require 4½ yards of material 22 inches wide, or 2⅜ yards 44 inches wide, or 1⅞ yard 54 inches wide.

FIGURE No 409 A.—LADIES' COSTUME.—This illustrates Ladies' costume No. 4737 (copyright), which is again shown on page 96 of this publication. The pattern is in 13 sizes for ladies from 28 to 46 inches, bust measure, and costs 1s. 8d. or 40 cents. For a lady of medium size, it will require 11½ yards of material 22 inches wide, or 5 yards 50 inches wide.

FIGURE No. 410 A.—LADIES' COSTUME.—This portrays Ladies' costume No. 4738 (copyright), again shown on page 96. The pattern is in 13 sizes for ladies from 28 to 46 inches, bust measure, and costs 1s. 8d. or 40 cents. Of one material for a lady of medium size, it needs 12½ yards 22 inches wide, or 6⅜ yards 44 inches wide, or 5¾ yards 50 inches wide.

4747   **4747**

No. 4747.—MISSES' BASQUE, WITH JACKET FRONT (Copyright).— The pattern of this stylishly devised basque is in 7 sizes for misses from 10 to 16 years of age. Of one material for a miss of 12 years, it requires 4⅛ yards 22 inches wide, or 2 yards 44 inches wide, or 1¾ yard 50 inches wide. In the combination seen, it needs 1⅞ yard of dress goods 40 inches wide, with ⅝ yard of silk and ½ yard of velvet each 20 inches wide. Price of pattern, 1s. or 25 cts.

4779   **4779**   **4779**

No. 4779.—LADIES' PRINCESS COSTUME, WITH BELL BACK, HAVING A SLIGHT TRAIN (PERFORATED FOR ROUND LENGTH) (Copyright).—Another view of this stylish costume is portrayed at figure No. 418 A on this page. The pattern is in 13 sizes for ladies from 28 to 46 inches, bust measure. For a lady of medium size, it requires 12⅜ yards of material 22 inches wide, or 6⅜ yards 44 inches wide, or 5½ yards 50 inches wide. Price of pattern, 1s. 8d. or 40 cents.

FIGURE NO. 434 A.—MISSES' GREEK COSTUME.—This illustrates Misses' costume No. 4756 (copyright), shown again on page 101. In the present instance vailing was used for the pretty gown, and spotted silk and lace provide a stylish trimming. All sorts of softly falling fabrics may be used for developing the mode, and lace or ribbon may supply garniture. The pattern is in 7 sizes for misses from 10 to 16 years of age, and costs 1s. 6d. or 35 cents. To make the costume for a miss of 12 years, will require 7⅝ yards of material 22 inches wide, or 3⅝ yards 44 inches wide. If goods 50 inches wide be chosen, then 3⅛ yards will suffice.

4770   **4770**

No. 4770.—LADIES' RUSSIAN BLOUSE (WITH FITTED LINING) (Copyright).—This pretty style of Russian blouse is shown differently made up at figure No. 421 A on page 100. Silk was here used for it, and it is becomingly trimmed with a jabot of the silk. The pattern is in 13 sizes for ladies from 28 to 46 inches, bust measure. For a lady of medium size, the garment requires 4⅞ yards of material 22 inches wide, or 2⅞ yards 44 inches wide, or 2⅜ yards 50 inches wide. Price of pattern, 1s. 3d. or 30 cents.

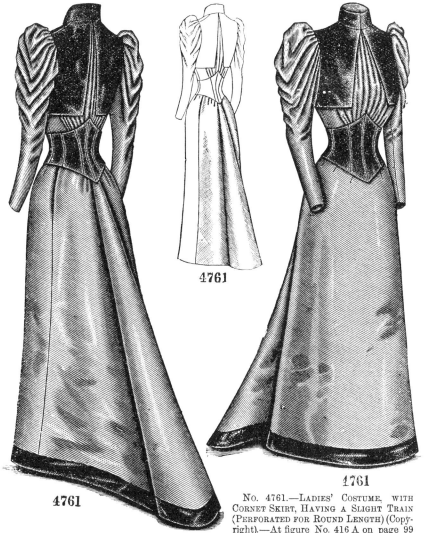

4761

4761

4761

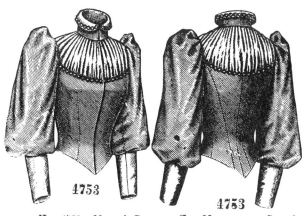

4753

4753

No. 4753.—Misses' Basque (In Marguerite Style) (Copyr't).—Another view of this modish basque is presented at figure No. 439 A on page 95. Woollen dress goods and silk are here united, with a simple arrangement of gimp for decoration. The pattern is in 9 sizes for misses from 8 to 16 years old. For a miss of 12 years, it requires 1¼ yard of dress goods 40 inches wide, with 1¼ yard of silk 20 inches wide. Of one material, it will need 3 yards 22 inches wide, or 1½ yard 44 inches wide. Price of pattern, 1s. or 25 cents.

No. 4761.—Ladies' Costume, with Cornet Skirt, Having a Slight Train (Perforated for Round Length) (Copyright).—At figure No. 416 A on page 99 this costume is again depicted. The pattern is in 13 sizes for ladies from 28 to 46 inches, bust measure. As illustrated for a lady of medium size, it requires 4⅞ yards of dress goods 40 inches wide, with 1⅜ yard of velvet. Of one material, it needs 9⅜ yards 22 inches wide, or 5 yards 44 inches wide, or 4½ yards 50 inches wide. Price of pattern, 1s. 8d. or 40 cents.

4785

4785

4785

No. 4785.—Ladies' Russian Basque (Copyright). — This basque is also shown at figure No. 415 A on page 95 of this publication. The garment will develop handsomely in cloth, faille, Bengaline, plissé, Bedford cord, camel's-hair etc., with fur, passementerie, Russian bands, gimp, jet, galloon or braid for decoration. The pattern is in 13 sizes for ladies from 28 to 46 inches, bust measure. To make the basque for a lady of medium size, will require 5 yards of material 22 inches wide, or 3⅛ yards 44 inches wide, or 2⅞ yards 50 inches wide. Price of pattern, 1s. 3d. or 30 cents.

Figure No. 449 A.—Girls' Dress.—This illustrates Girls' dress No. 4778 (copyright), pictured on page 96. The pattern is in 8 sizes for girls from 5 to 12 years of age, and costs 1s. or 25 cents. Of one material for a girl of 8 years, it needs 4¾ yards 22 inches wide, or 3⅝ yards 30 inches wide, or 2⅜ yards 44 inches wide.

No. 4777.—Girls' Dress (Copyright).—At figure No. 448 A on page 98 this picturesque dress is shown differently made up. A plain variety of woollen dress goods was here chosen for it, and fancy braid forms the garniture. The pattern is in 8 sizes for girls from 5 to 12 years of age, and will make up handsomely in cashmere, challis, merino, serge, gingham and wash silks. For a girl of 8 years, it needs 5½ yards of material 22 inches wide, or 4¼ yards 30 inches wide, or 2⅝ yards 44 inches wide. Price of pattern, 1s. or 25 cents.

4777

4777

4752

No. 4752.—Ladies' Sleeve, with Deep Cuff (For Street Garments) (Copyright).—This pattern is in 7 sizes for ladies from 9 to 15 inches, arm measure, measuring the arm about an inch below the bottom of the arm's-eye. For a lady whose arm measures 11 inches as described, a pair of sleeves needs ⅝ yard of cloth 54 inches wide, with ⅝ yard of velvet 20 inches wide. Of one material, it requires 1⅞ yard 22 inches wide, or 1⅛ yard 44 inches wide, or 1 yard 54 inches wide. Price of pattern, 5d. or 10 cts.

Figure No. 427 A.—Ladies' Russian Cloak.—This is Ladies' Russian cloak No. 4758 (copyr't), seen on page 102. The pattern is in 10 sizes for ladies from 28 to 46 inches, bust measure, and costs 1s. 8d. or 40 cents. For a lady of medium size, it needs 7 yards of goods 36 inches wide, or 6 yards 44 inches wide, or 5 yards 54 inches wide.

Figure No. 416 A.—Ladies' Costume.—This portrays Ladies' costume No. 4761 (copyright), shown on page 97. The pattern is in 13 sizes for ladies from 28 to 46 ins., bust meas., and costs 1s. 8d. or 40 cts. Of one material for a lady of medium size, it needs 9⅜ yds. 22 ins. wide, or 5 yds. 44 ins. wide, or 4½ yds. 50 ins. wide.

1773   **1773**

No. 4773.—Misses' Wrapper (With Fitted Under-Front) (Copyright). —This comfortable wrapper is differently illustrated at figure No. 438 A on page 100. Blue-and-white striped French flannel was used for it in this instance, and ribbon trims it simply. The pattern is in 7 sizes for misses from 10 to 16 years of age. To make the garment for a miss of 12 years, requires $5\frac{7}{8}$ yards of goods 22 inches wide, or $4\frac{3}{4}$ yards 30 inches wide, or $3\frac{1}{4}$ yards 44 inches wide. Price of pattern, 1s. 3d. or 30 cents.

Figure No. 419 A.—Ladies' Evening Waist.—This illustrates Ladies' waist No. 4788 (copyright), shown on page 97 of this publication. The pattern is in 13 sizes for ladies from 28 to 46 inches, bust measure, and costs 1s. or 25 cents. To make the waist for a lady of medium size, will require 3 yards of goods 22 inches wide, or $2\frac{3}{4}$ yards 30 inches wide, or $1\frac{7}{8}$ yard 44 inches wide. In the combination illustrated on page 97, it needs $2\frac{7}{8}$ yards of lace net 27 inches wide, with $2\frac{3}{8}$ yards of silk 20 inches wide.

4771   **4771**

No. 4771.—Ladies' Wrapper or Lounging-Robe (Copyright).—This dainty and comfortable lounging-robe is represented in a different development at figure No. 426 A on page 101 of this publication. The pattern is in 11 sizes for ladies from 28 to 48 inches, bust measure. To make the garment for a lady of medium size, will require $9\frac{1}{4}$ yards of goods 22 inches wide, or 8 yards 27 inches wide, or $6\frac{3}{8}$ yards 36 inches wide, or 5 yards 44 inches wide. Price of pattern, 1s. 6d. or 35 cents.

4754

No. 4754.— Misses' Rus- sian Coat, with Wat- teau Back (Copyright).— A different representation of this stylish coat may be seen at figure No. 442 A on page 97. Plain

4751   **4754**

cloth was here used for the coat, and machine-stitching provides an edge finish and outlines a cuff on each sleeve. The pattern is in 7 sizes for misses from 10 to 16 years of age. For a miss of 12 years, it calls for $4\frac{1}{2}$ yards of material 22 inches wide, or $2\frac{3}{8}$ yards 44 inches wide, or $1\frac{7}{8}$ yard 54 inches wide. Price of pattern, 1s. 3d. or 30 cents.

No. 4744.—
Little Girls'
Cloak (Copy-
right). — This
pattern, seen
in a different
development
at figure No.
455 A on page
98, is in 7
sizes for little
girls from ½
to 6 years of
age. To make
the cloak for a
girl of 5 years,
will require
5½ yards of
material 22 in-
ches wide, or 2⅝ yards 44 inches wide, or 2½ yards
54 inches wide. Price of pattern, 10d. or 20 cents.

4744   **4744**

No. 4790.
—Child's
Coat (Copy-
right). — This
coat is differ-
ently pictured
at figure No.
451 A on this
page. It is here
shown made
of cloth a n d
trimmed with
fur. The pat-
tern is in 7
sizes for chil-
dren from ½
to 6 years old.
For a child of
5 years, it re-
quires 5 yards
of goods 22 inches wide, or 2½ yards 44 inches wide,
or 2⅛ yards 54 inches wide. Price, 10d. or 20 cents.

4790   **4790**

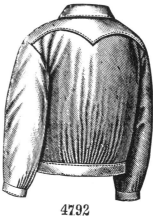

4792   **4792**

No. 4792.—Men's Jumper or Working Blouse.—Gingham is
the material represented in this blouse, and machine-stitching furnishes a neat completion. Denim, cotton cheviot and plain and fancy
gingham are appropriate for garments of this kind, and the finish
will be as illustrated. The pattern is in 10 sizes for men from 32 to
50 inches, breast measure. To make the garment for a man of
medium size, requires 3¾ yards of material 27 inches wide, or
2⅞ yards 36 inches wide. Price of pattern, 10d. or 20 cents.

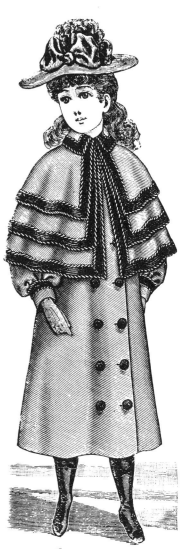

Figure No. 443 A.—Girls' Watteau Coat.
— This represents Girls' Watteau coat No. 4765
(copyright), which is again pictured on page
95. The pattern is in 10 sizes for girls from 3
to 12 years of age, and costs 1s. 3d. or 30 cts.
To make the coat of one material for a girl of
8 years, will call for 6 yards 22 inches wide,
or 3⅜ yards 44 inches wide. If 54-inch-wide
goods be chosen, then 3 yards will suffice.

4791   **4791**

No. 4791.—Men's Inverness Overcoat.—This stylish
overcoat is pictured made of fine all-wool corkscrew. The
pattern is in 10 sizes for men from 32 to 50 inches, breast
measure. To make the garment for a man of medium
size, will call for 6⅛ yards of material 27 inches wide, or
3 yards 54 inches wide. Price of pattern, 1s. 6d. or 35 cents.

Figure No. 444 A.—Girls' Cloak.
—This illustrates Girls' cloak No.
4783 (copyr't), again shown on page
101. The pattern is in 10 sizes for
girls from 3 to 12 years old, and costs
1s. 3d. or 30 cents. For a girl of 8
years, it needs 6⅝ yards of goods 22
inches wide, or 3⅝ yards 44 inches
wide. If goods 54 inches wide be
selected, then 2⅞ yards will suffice.

No. 4788.—LADIES' EVENING WAIST (Copyright). — At figure No. 419 A on page 100 this stylish waist may be seen differently developed. The waist is here shown made of lace net over silk and prettily trimmed with ribbon. The pattern is in 13 sizes for ladies from 28 to 46 inches, bust measure. For a lady of medium size, it requires 2⅞ yards of lace net 27 inches wide, with 2⅜ yards of silk 20 inches wide. Of one material, it calls for 3 yards 22 inches wide, or 2¾ yards 30 inches wide, or 1⅞ yard 44 inches wide. Price of pattern, 1s. or 25 cents.

4788

4788

FIGURE NO. 451 A.—CHILD'S TOILETTE.—This consists of Child's coat No. 4790 (copyright), shown on this page; and cap No. 2989 (copyright), on page 63. The coat pattern is in 7 sizes for children from ½ to 6 years of age, and costs 10d. or 20 cents. The cap pattern is in 4 sizes for children from 1 to 7 years old, and costs 5d. or 10 cents. For a child of 5 years, the coat requires 5 yards of material 22 inches wide, and the cap ⅜ yard, with ⅜ yard of silk to line.

4796

No. 4796.— MISSES' BASQUE (KNOWN AS THE MARGUERITE BASQUE) (Copyr't). —This basque is again depicted at figure No. 440 A on page 95. The pattern is in 7 sizes for misses from 10 to 16 years of age. In the combination shown for a miss of 12 years, it will require ⅞ yard of dress goods 40 inches wide, with 3⅜ yards of silk. Of one material, it needs 4 yards 22 inches wide, or 2 yards 44 ins. wide, or 1⅝ yard 50 inches wide. Price of pattern, 1s. or 25 cents.

4796

4817

4817

4817

4817

No. 4817.— LADIES' HOODS (Copyright). — This pattern is in 3 sizes—small, medium and large.

In the medium size, the hood with revers needs ¾ yard of goods 22 inches wide, or ⅝ yard 27 inches or more wide, with ¾ yard of silk to line. The hood without revers needs ⅝ yard 22 inches or more wide, with ⅝ yard of silk to line. Price of pattern, 7d. or 15 cents.

FIGURE NO. 454 A.—LITTLE GIRLS' DRESS.—This illustrates Little Girls' dress No. 4786 (copyright), which is differently represented on page 101 of this publication. In the present instance spotted silk is the material pictured in the becoming little dress, with ribbon for decoration. The pattern is in 9 sizes for little girls from ½ to 8 years of age, and costs 10d. or 20 cents. For a little girl of 5 years, it calls for 5 yards of material 22 inches wide, or 4⅛ yards 27 inches wide, or 2⅞ yards 36 inches wide. Of 44-inch-wide goods, 2⅜ yards will suffice.

4763

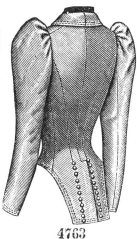

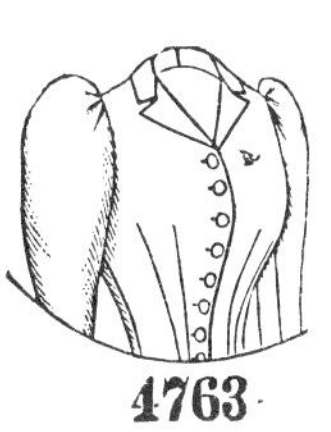

4763

No. 4763.— LADIES' BASQUE (TO BE MADE WITH OR WITHOUT A CHEMISETTE) (Copyright). — This pattern, which is again shown at figure No. 422 A on page 101, is in 14 sizes for ladies from 28 to 48 inches, bust measure. To make the basque for a lady of medium size, will require 2 yards of dress goods 40 inches wide, and ¾ yard of velvet. Of one material, it needs 4¼ yards 22 inches wide, or 2⅛ yards 44 inches wide, or 1¾ yard 50 inches wide. Price of pattern, 1s. 3d. or 30 cents.

FIGURE NO. 405 A.—LADIES' BASQUE.—This portrays Ladies' basque No. 4795 (copyright), also pictured on page 97. A different illustration of the basque is given at figure No. 406 A on page 102. The pattern is in 13 sizes for ladies from 28 to 46 inches, bust measure, and costs 1s. 3d. or 30 cents. Of one material for a lady of medium size, the garment requires 4⅜ yards 22 inches wide, or 2⅜ yards 44 inches wide, or 2 yards 50 inches wide.

FIGURE NO. 452 A.—LITTLE GIRLS' TOILETTE.—This consists of Little Girls' Granny cloak No. 4768 (copyr't), and bonnet No. 4748 (copyr't), both shown on page 100. The cloak pattern is in 7 sizes for little girls from 1 to 7 years of age, and costs 10d. or 20 cents. The bonnet pattern is in 4 sizes from 1 to 7 years, and costs 5d. or 10 cents. Of one material for a girl of 5 years, the cloak needs 4⅜ yards 22 inches wide, or 2¼ yards 44 inches wide, or 1¾ yard 54 inches wide. The bonnet requires ⅜ yard 20 inches or more wide, with ¾ yard of Surah, and ⅜ yard of lining silk.

FIGURE NO. 438 A.—MISSES' WRAPPER.—This illustrates Misses' wrapper No. 4773 (copyright), shown again on page 98. The wrapper is here pictured developed in figured cashmere and daintily trimmed with satin ribbon ruchings and ribbons. The pattern is in 7 sizes for misses from 10 to 16 years of age, and costs 1s. 3d. or 30 cents. To make the wrapper for a miss of 12 years, will require 5⅞ yards of material 22 inches wide, or 4¾ yards 30 inches wide, or 3¼ yards 44 inches wide.

4787 **4787**

No. 4787.—CHILD'S NIGHT-GOWN.—Muslin was used for making the night-gown pictured in the above engravings, and embroidered edging furnishes the trimming. The pattern is in 9 sizes for children from 1 to 9 years of age. To make the garment for a child of 5 years, will require 4⅛ yards of goods 22 inches wide, or 3⅜ yards 27 inches wide. If material 36 inches wide be chosen, then 2½ yards will prove amply sufficient. Price of pattern, 10d. or 20 cents.

4768 **4768**

No. 4768.—LITTLE GIRLS' GRANNY CLOAK, WITH YOKE AND COLLAR (Copyright).—By referring to figure No. 452 A on page 99, this cloak may be seen differently made up. Faille, Bengaline, serge, camel's-hair, flannel or Bedford cord may be chosen for the cloak, with stitching, lace or embroidery for decoration. The pattern is in 7 sizes for little girls from 1 to 7 years of age. For a girl of 5 years, it will require 4⅜ yards of goods 22 inches wide, or 2¼ yards 44 inches wide, or 1¾ yard 54 inches wide. Price of pattern, 10d. or 20 cents.

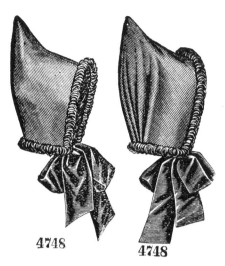

4748   4748

No. 4748.—LITTLE GIRLS' BONNET (Copyright).—This bonnet is also pictured at figures Nos. 450 A on page 98 and 452 A on page 99. The pattern is in 4 sizes for little girls from 1 to 7 years old. For a girl of 5 years, it needs $\frac{3}{8}$ yard of material 20 inches or more in width, with $\frac{3}{4}$ yard of Surah and $\frac{3}{8}$ yard of lining silk. Price of pattern, 5d. or 10 cents.

FIGURE NO. 450 A.—LITTLE GIRLS' TOILETTE.—This consists of Little Girls' cloak No. 4784 (copyright), again depicted on page 97; and bonnet No. 4748 (copyright), shown on page 100. The cloak pattern is in 7 sizes for little girls from $\frac{1}{2}$ to 6 years old, and costs 10d. or 20 cents. The bonnet pattern is in 4 sizes for little girls from 1 to 7 years old, and costs 5d. or 10 cents. For a girl of 5 years, the cloak requires $4\frac{3}{4}$ yards of material 22 inches wide, or $2\frac{1}{2}$ yards 44 inches wide. The bonnet calls for $\frac{3}{8}$ yard of goods 20 inches or more in width, with $\frac{3}{4}$ yard of Surah, and $\frac{3}{8}$ yard of lining silk.

FIGURE NO. 421 A.—LADIES' TOILETTE.—This consists of Ladies' Russian blouse No. 4770 (copyr't), shown on page 98; and girdle No. 4745 (copyr't), pictured on page 95. For sizes, prices, and quantities of goods needed refer to pages 95 and 98.

4757

No. 4757.—MISSES' AND GIRLS' SLEEVE, WITH DEEP CUFF (FOR STREET GARMENTS) (Copyright). —A pretty and effective combination of velvet and cloth is pictured in this sleeve. The pattern is in 8 sizes from 2 to 16 years of age. To make a pair of sleeves for a miss of 12 years, will need $\frac{5}{8}$ yard of cloth 54 inches wide, with $\frac{1}{2}$ yard of velvet 20 inches wide. Of one material, it needs $1\frac{3}{4}$ yard 22 inches wide, or 1 yard 44 inches wide, or $\frac{7}{8}$ yard 54 inches wide. Price of pattern, 5d. or 10 cts.

FIGURE NO. 437 A. — MISSES' TOILETTE.— This consists of Misses' Russian basque No. 4793 (copyr't). seen on page 96; and Corselet Princess skirt No. 4725 (copyright), on page 91. Both patterns are in 7 sizes for misses from 10 to 16 years of age: the basque costing 1s. or 25 cents; and the skirt, 1s. 3d. or 30 cents. For a miss of 12 years, they need $4\frac{1}{2}$ yards of goods 44 inches wide: the basque needing $2\frac{1}{4}$ yards; and the skirt, $2\frac{1}{4}$ yards.

4794

No. 4794.—Ladies' Legging and Over-Gaiter (Copyright).—This pattern is in 5 sizes for shoe numbers from 2 to 6, or from 13 to 17 inches, calf measure. For a lady wearing a No. 4 shoe, or whose calf measures 15 inches, a pair of leggings will need $\frac{5}{8}$ yard of goods 54 inches wide, with a piece of leather 2x5 inches for the straps; while a pair of over-gaiters requires $\frac{1}{4}$ yard 54 inches wide, with a piece of leather 2x5 inches for the straps. Price of pattern, 7d. or 15 cts.

4742   **4742**

No. 4742.—Girls' Apron (Copyright).—This apron is again pictured at figure No. 447 A on page 95. The pattern is in 8 sizes for girls from 5 to 12 years of age. For a girl of 8 years, it needs 2 yards of lawn 36 inches wide, with 1 yard of embroidered edging $3\frac{1}{2}$ inches wide, and $\frac{3}{4}$ yard of insertion 2 inches wide. Of one material, it requires $2\frac{3}{4}$ yards 27 inches wide, or 2 yards 36 inches wide. Price of pattern, 10d. or 20 cents.

Figure No. 506 A.—Child's Toilette.—This consists of Child's dress No. 4798 (copyright), shown on page 104; and girls' guimpe No. 4478 (copyright), on page 52. The dress pattern is in 8 sizes for children from $\frac{1}{2}$ to 7 years of age, and costs 10d. or 20 cents. The guimpe pattern is in 11 sizes from 2 to 12 years old, and costs 5d. or 10 cents. For a child of 5 years, the dress requires $4\frac{3}{4}$ yards of goods 22 inches wide, and the guimpe $3\frac{1}{2}$ yards of goods in the same width.

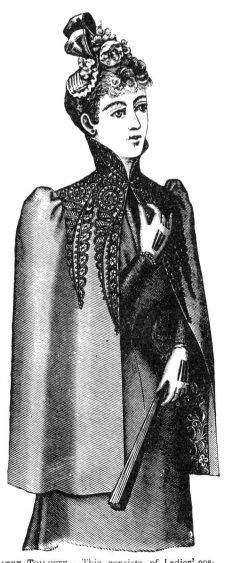

Figure No. 485 A.—Ladies' Toilette.—This consists of Ladies' basque No. 4856 (copyr't,) seen on page 104; and skirt No. 4816 (copyr't), on page 109. The basque pattern is in 13 sizes for ladies from 28 to 46 inches, bust meas., and costs 1s. 3d. or 30 cts. The skirt pattern is in 11 sizes for ladies from 20 to 40 ins., waist meas., and costs 1s. 6d. or 35 cts. For goods needed, see pages 104 and 109.

Figure No. 486 A.—Ladies' Theatre Toilette.—This consists of Ladies' costume No. 4805 (copyright), shown on page 108; and cape No. 4850 (copyright), on page 104. The costume pattern is in 13 sizes for ladies from 28 to 46 ins., bust measure, and costs 1s. 8d. or 40 cts. The cape pattern is in 10 sizes from 28 to 46 inches, bust measure, and costs 1s. or 25 cents. For goods needed, see pages 104 and 108.

4783   4783

No. 4783.—Girls' Cloak (Copyright).—This pattern, shown at figure No. 444 A on page 99, is in 10 sizes for girls from 3 to 12 years old. For a girl of 8 years, it requires 6⅝ yards of goods 22 inches wide, or 3⅝ yards 44 inches wide, or 2⅞ yds. 54 ins. wide. Price, 1s. 3d. or 30 cts.

Set No. 151.—Girl Dolls' Dress, Guimpe and Cloak (Copyright).—At figure No. 515 A on page 104 the guimpe and dress of this Set are again shown. The Set is in 7 sizes for girl dolls from 12 to 24 inches tall. For a doll 22 inches tall, the dress and cloak need 1¾ yard of cashmere 40 inches wide, and the guimpe ⅝ yard of silk 20 inches wide. Price of Set, 10d. or 20 cents.

Figure No. 468 A.—Ladies' Princess Costume.—This is Ladies' costume No. 4829 (copyright), again pictured on page 107. The pattern is in 13 sizes for ladies from 28 to 46 inches, bust measure, and costs 1s. 8d. or 40 cents. For a lady of medium size, it requires 11½ yards of material 22 inches wide.

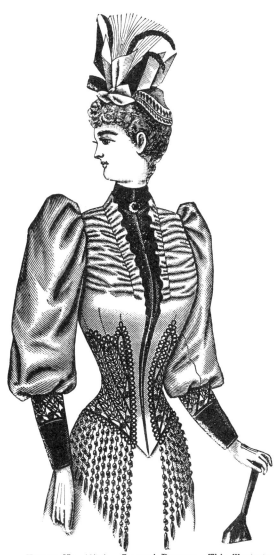

Figure No. 487 A.—Ladies' Basque.—This illustrates Ladies' basque No. 4802 (copyright), shown again on page 108. The pattern is in 13 sizes for ladies from 28 to 46 inches. bust measure, and costs 1s. 3d. or 30 cents. To make the basque for a lady of medium size, requires 4⅛ yards of material 22 inches wide, or 2¼ yards 44 inches wide, or 2 yards 50 inches wide.

4756

4756

No. 4756.—MISSES' GREEK COSTUME (KNOWN AS THE HYPATIA GOWN) (Copyright).—This costume is again shown at figure No. 434 A on page 98. It may be made with or without the coat sleeves and with a high or low neck, as preferred. White challis is the material here represented, with a Greek-key design done with gold braid for decoration. The pattern is in 7 sizes for misses from 10 to 16 years of age. For a miss of 12 years, it needs 7⅝ yards of goods 22 inches wide, or 3⅝ yards 44 inches wide, or 3⅛ yards 50 inches wide. Price of pattern, 1s. 6d. or 35 cents.

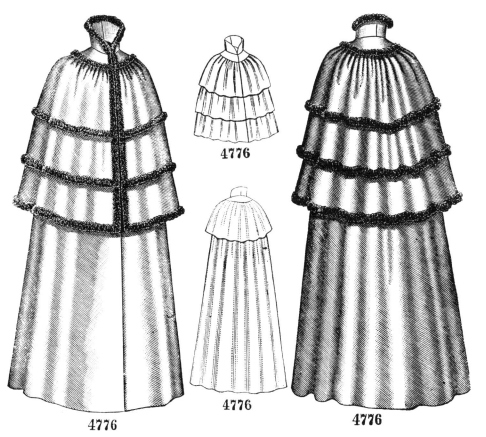

4776

4776

4776

No. 4776.—MISSES' LONG WRAP. (TO BE MADE WITH ONE, TWO OR THREE CAPES) (Copyright).—This notably graceful wrap is represented made of light cloth, lined with fancy silk and trimmed with fur binding at figure No. 402 A on page 96 of this publication. Fawn cloth was used for its development in the present instance, and bands of fur trim it attractively. The pattern is in 7 sizes for misses from 10 to 16 years old. For a miss of 12 years, it needs 9⅛ yards of goods 22 inches wide, or 5 yards 44 inches wide. If material 54 inches wide be chosen, then 4⅛ yards will prove sufficient. Price of pattern, 1s. 6d. or 35 cents.

FIGURE No. 426 A.—LADIES' WRAPPER.—This illustrates Ladies' wrapper No. 4771 (copyright), pictured on page 99. The pattern is in 11 sizes for ladies from 28 to 48 inches, bust measure, and costs 1s. 6d. or 35 cents. Of one material for a lady of medium size, it needs 9¼ yards 22 inches wide, or 8 yards 27 inches wide, or 6⅜ yards 36 inches wide, or 5 yards 44 inches wide.

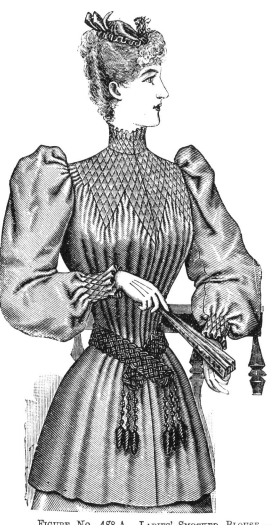

4786   4786

No. 4786.—Little Girls' Dress, with Medium-Short Waist (Copyright).—This simple frock is pictured made of a different material and otherwise trimmed at figure No. 454 A on page 99. It will make up prettily in all kinds of dress goods, and soft silk, ribbon, lace, feather-stitching, etc., will provide pretty garniture. The pattern is in 9 sizes for little girls from ½ to 8 years of age. For a girl of 5 years, it needs 5 yards of goods 22 inches wide, or 4⅛ yards 27 inches wide, or 2⅞ yards 36 inches wide, or 2⅜ yards 44 inches wide. Price of pattern, 10d. or 20 cents.

Figure No. 488 A.—Ladies' Smocked Blouse.—This illustrates Ladies' blouse No. 4820 (copyright), shown again on page 107. The pattern is in 13 sizes for ladies from 28 to 46 inches, bust measure, and costs 1s. 3d. or 30 cents. To make the blouse for a lady of medium size, needs 5⅝ yards of goods 22 inches wide.

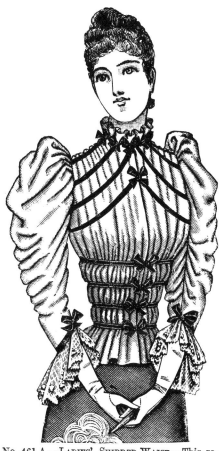

Figure No. 461 A.—Ladies' Shirred Waist.—This represents Ladies' waist No. 4854 (copyright), again illustrated on page 108. The pattern is in 11 sizes for ladies from 28 to 42 inches, bust measure, and costs 1s. or 25 cents. For a lady of medium size, it needs 4¾ yards of goods 22 inches wide, or 2¾ yards 44 ins. wide, or 2⅜ yards 50 ins. wide.

4855   4855

No. 4855.—Ladies' Double-Breasted Coat (In Three-Quarter Length) (Copyright).—By referring to figure No. 456 A on page 106 of this issue, another illustration of this stylish top-garment may be observed. The pattern is in 13 sizes for ladies from 28 to 46 inches, bust measure, and will make up nicely in all seasonable varieties of coatings, fur, braid, silk or mohair binding or machine-stitching providing the finish. To make the garment for a lady of medium size, requires 6½ yards of material 22 inches wide, or 3⅜ yards 44 inches wide, or 2⅝ yards 54 inches wide. Price of pattern, 1s. 6d. or 35 cts.

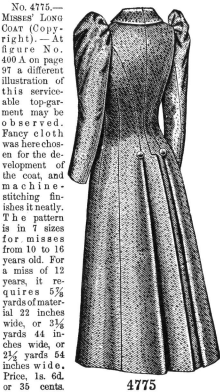

No. 4775.—Misses' Long Coat (Copyright).—At figure No. 400 A on page 97 a different illustration of this serviceable top-garment may be observed. Fancy cloth was here chosen for the development of the coat, and machine-stitching finishes it neatly. The pattern is in 7 sizes for misses from 10 to 16 years old. For a miss of 12 years, it requires 5⅞ yards of material 22 inches wide, or 3⅛ yards 44 inches wide, or 2½ yards 54 inches wide. Price, 1s. 6d. or 35 cents.

4775   4775

4739

No. 4739. — MISSES' WATTEAU COAT (Copyright). — This garment is again pictured at figure No. 401 A on page 97. It is here illustrated made of cloth and trimmed with fur. Any plain or fancy cloaking of either smooth or rough surface will develop styl-

4739

4739

ishly by the mode, and a plain finish may be adopted if desired. The pattern is in 7 sizes for misses from 10 to 16 years of age. To make the garment for a miss of 12 years, will require 4⅝ yards of material 22 inches wide, or 2¾ yards 44 inches wide, or 2¼ yards 54 inches wide. Price of pattern, 1s. 3d. or 30 cents.

FIGURE No. 423 A.—LADIES' OUTDOOR TOILETTE.— This consists of Ladies' long coat No. 4759 (copyr't), shown on page 102; skirt No. 4631 (copyr't), on page 83; and basque No. 4348 (copyr't), on page 37. The coat pattern is in 13 sizes for ladies from 28 to 46 ins., bust measure, and costs 1s. 8d. or 40 cts. The skirt pattern is in 9 sizes for ladies from 20 to 36 ins., waist meas., and costs 1s. 6d. or 35 cts. The basque pattern is in 14 sizes for ladies from 28 to 48 ins., bust meas., and costs 1s. 3d. or 30 cts. For a lady of medium size, they will need 9¾ yards of material 44 inches wide.

4764

No. 4764.— GIRLS' COAT (Copyright). — Rough-surfaced coating was employed for this coat, and buttons provide an appropriate finish. Cloth, melton, and plain or fancy coating of seasonable texture are popular for top garments for girls, and machine-stitching, fur bands, or bindings of braid may be chosen for an edge finish. The collar and pocket-laps may be of velvet. The pattern is in 10 sizes for girls from 3 to 12 years old. For a girl of 8 years, it needs 5⅜ yards of material 22 inches wide, or 2⅝ yards 44 inches wide. If goods 54 inches wide be chosen, then 2⅛ yards will suffice. Price of pattern, 1s. or 25 cents.

4764

4764

4766

No. 4766.— LADIES' COAT (SUITABLE FOR SEALSKIN, PLUSH, ETC.) (Copyr't). — This coat may be again seen by referring to figure No. 431 A elsewhere on this page. The coat is fashionably loose-fitting in effect and is here portrayed made of seal-plush. The closing is made with cord loops over olive buttons, but any preferred style of buttons may be used. The pattern is in 10 sizes for ladies from 28 to 46 inches, bust measure. For a lady of medium size, it needs 5¼ yards of goods 22 inches wide, or 2⅞ yards 44 inches wide, or 2¼ yards 50 inches wide, or 2⅛ yards 54 inches wide. Price of pattern, 1s. 6d. or 35 cents.

4766

4766

SET NO. 153.—LADY DOLLS' BELL SKIRT, RUSSIAN BLOUSE AND WRAP (Copyright).— The skirt and wrap of this Set, are again pictured at figure No. 513 A on page 109. The Set is in 7 sizes for dolls from 12 to 24 inches tall. For a doll 22 inches tall, the skirt and blouse need 1⅛ yard of dress goods 40 inches wide, and the wrap, ⅞ yard of cloth 54 inches wide. Price of Set, 10d. or 20 cents.

FIGURE NO. 431 A.—LADIES' COAT.—This illustrates Ladies' coat No. 4766 (copyright), shown on this page. The pattern is in 10 sizes for ladies from 28 to 46 inches, bust measure, and costs 1s. 6d. or 35 cents. For a lady of medium size, the coat will require 5¼ yards of material 22 inches wide, or 2⅞ yards 44 inches wide, or 2¼ yards 50 inches wide, or 2⅛ yards 54 inches wide.

FIGURE NO. 432 A.—LADIES TOILETTE.—This consists of Ladies' double-breasted vest No. 4751 (copyright), again portrayed on page 97: and Eton jacket No. 4634 (copyright), on page 82. Both patterns are in 13 sizes for ladies from 28 to 46 inches, bust measure: the vest costing 10d. or 20 cents; and the jacket, 1s. or 25 cents. To make the toilette for a lady of medium size, will require 2½ yards of goods 44 inches wide, the vest needing ⅞ yard, and the jacket, 1⅝ yard.

4849 **4849**

NO. 4849.—LADIES' DOUBLE-BREASTED WATTEAU COAT (IN THREE-QUARTER LENGTH) (Copyright).—This pattern, also shown at figure No. 457 A on page 110, is in 13 sizes for ladies from 28 to 46 inches, bust measure. For a lady of medium size, the coat requires 2¾ yards of cloth 54 inches wide, with a piece of fur measuring 22 x 49¾ inches. Of one material, it needs 8⅛ yards 22 inches wide. Price of pattern, 1s. 6d. or 35 cents.

FIGURE No 515 A.—
GIRL DOLLS' TOILETTE.—
This consists of the dress
and guimpe included in
Girl Dolls' Set No. 151
(copyr't), pictured in full
on page 103. The Set is
in 7 sizes for girl dolls
from 12 to 24 inches tall,
and costs 10d. or 20 cts.
For amount of goods re-
quired, see page 103.

FIGURE NO. 425 A.—LADIES' HOUSE TOILETTE.—This
consists of Ladies' tea-jacket No. 4780 (copyright), seen
on page 98; and bell skirt No. 4728 (copyright), on
page 88. The jacket pattern is in 13 sizes for ladies
from 28 to 46 inches, bust measure, and costs 1s. 3d.
or 30 cents. The skirt pattern is in 9 sizes for
ladies from 20 to 36 inches, waist measure, and
costs 1s. 6d. or 35 cents. For a lady of medium size,
they need 11¾ yards of material 22 inches wide.

FIGURE NO. 453 A.—CHILD'S DRESS.—
This illustrates Child's dress No. 4749
(copyright), which is shown in a different
development on page 95. Blue India silk
is here pictured in the dress, with ribbon
in the same shade, and lace for decoration.
The pattern is in 7 sizes for children from
½ to 6 years of age, and costs 10d. or 20
cents. For a child of 5 years, it needs
4 yards of material 22 inches wide, or
3½ yards 27 inches wide, or 2½ yards
36 inches wide, or 2 yards 44 inches wide.

FIGURE NO. 406 A.—LADIES' RECEPTION TOILETTE.—This consists of Ladies' basque No. 4795 (copyr't), again portrayed on
page 97; and trained skirt No. 4734 (copyr't), on page 88. The basque pattern is in 13 sizes for ladies from 28 to 46 inches, bust
measure, and costs 1s. 3d. or 30 cents. The skirt pattern is in 9 sizes for ladies from 20 to 36 inches, waist measure, and costs
1s. 8d. or 40 cents. For a lady of medium size, they need 6⅞ yards of material 44 inches wide; the basque calling for 2⅜ yards,
and the skirt for 4½ yards. Of 50-inch-wide goods 6½ yards will suffice: the basque needing 2 yards; and the skirt, 4½ yards.

NO. 4760.—MISSES' LONG COAT, WITH WATTEAU BACK (Copyr't).—A dark shade of tan cloth was chosen for making this comfortable garment, and fur and machine-stitching form a rich trimming. The Watteau top-garments are among the season's latest novelties and are very popular. The mode will develop charmingly in all kinds of seasonable coatings, and any simple decoration may be added. The pattern is in 7 sizes for misses from 10 to 16 years of age. For a miss of 12 years, it needs 7⅞ yards of goods 22 inches wide, or 3¾ yards 44 inches wide or 3 yards 54 inches wide. Price of pattern, 1s. 6d. or 35 cents.

4760

4760

4798

4798

NO. 4798.—CHILD'S DRESS (PINAFORE DRESS) (Copyright).—This dress is shown at figure No. 506 A on page 103. The pattern is in 8 sizes for children from ½ to 7 years old. As pictured for a child of 5 years, it needs 2⅛ yards of dress goods 40 inches wide, and ½ yard of velvet. Of one material, the garment requires 4¾ yards 22 inches wide. Price of pattern, 10d. or 20 cents.

4759

4759

NO. 4759.—LADIES' LONG COAT, WITH WATTEAU BACK (Copyright).—This stylish coat is again depicted at figure No. 423 A on page 101. The pattern is in 13 sizes for ladies from 28 to 46 inches, bust measure. For a lady of medium size, it requires 11⅛ yards of material 22 inches wide, or 5¼ yards 44 inches wide, or 4⅝ yards 54 inches wide. Price of pattern, 1s. 8d. or 40 cents.

4743

4743

4743

NO. 4743.—LADIES' RUSSIAN COSTUME, WITH A SLIGHT TRAIN (PERFORATED FOR ROUND LENGTH) (Copyright).—Another representation of this costume may be seen at figure No. 414 A on page 96. Cloth and velvet are here combined in the costume, and jet passementerie and velvet trim it. The pattern is in 13 sizes for ladies from 28 to 46 inches, bust measure. For a lady of medium size, it needs 5 yards of cloth 50 inches wide, with 2 yards of velvet. Of one material, it needs 12⅛ yards 22 inches wide, or 6¼ yards 44 inches wide, or 5⅛ yards 50 inches wide. Price of pattern, 1s. 8d. or 40 cents.

4830

4830

4830

No. 4830.—LADIES' COSTUME, WITH A SLIGHT TRAIN (PERFORATED FOR ROUND LENGTH) (Copyright).—This pattern is in 13 sizes for ladies from 28 to 46 inches, bust measure. In the combination pictured for a lady of medium size, the costume requires 4⅞ yards of dress goods 40 inches wide, with 1¼ yard of velvet 20 inches wide. To make the costume of one material, will call for 9¾ yards 22 inches wide, or 5⅛ yards 44 inches wide, or 4¾ yards 50 inches wide. Price of pattern, 1s. 8d. or 40 cents.

4831

4831

No. 4831.—LADIES' BASQUE, WITH ATTACHED FULL SKIRT (Copyright).—This pattern, shown at figure No. 484 A on page 107, is in 13 sizes for ladies from 28 to 46 inches, bust measure. For a lady of medium size, it requires 2⅞ yards of dress goods 40 inches wide, with 2 yards of silk. Of one material, it needs 7 yards 22 inches wide, or 3½ yards 44 ins. wide, or 3 yds. 50 ins. wide. Price, 1s. 3d. or 30 cts.

FIGURE NO. 471 A.—LADIES' WATTEAU COSTUME.—This is Ladies' costume No. 4804 (copyright), shown on page 105. The pattern is in 13 sizes for ladies from 28 to 46 inches, bust measure, and costs 1s. 8d. or 40 cents. For a lady of medium size, it needs 9⅜ yards of goods 22 inches wide.

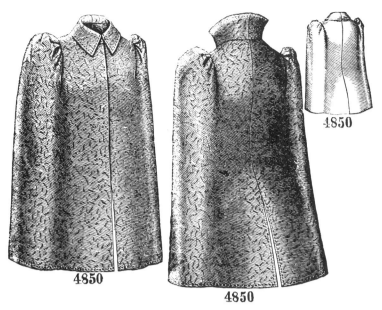

No. 4850.—LADIES' CAPE (Copyright).—This serviceable cape may be again seen at figure No. 486 A on page 103 of this publication. The pattern is in 10 sizes for ladies from 28 to 46 inches, bust measure. To make the cape for a lady of medium size, requires 3¼ yards of material 22 inches wide, or 2 yards 44 inches wide, or 2 yards 54 inches wide. Price of pattern, 1s. or 25 cents.

FIGURE No. 422 A.—LADIES' BASQUE.— This illustrates Ladies' basque No. 4763 (copyright), which is again portrayed on page 96 of this publication. The basque is here shown worn with a chemisette, but it may be omitted if deemed undesirable. The pattern is in 14 sizes for ladies from 28 to 48 inches, bust measure, and costs 1s. 3d. or 30 cents. As shown on page 96, for a lady of medium size, it requires 2 yards of dress goods 40 inches wide, with ¾ yard of velvet 20 inches wide. To make the basque of one material, will require 4¼ yards 22 inches wide, or 2⅛ yards 44 inches wide, or 1¾ yard 50 inches wide.

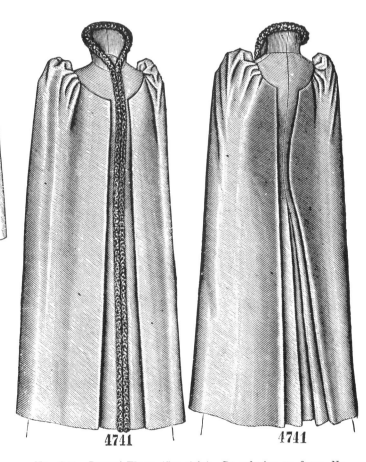

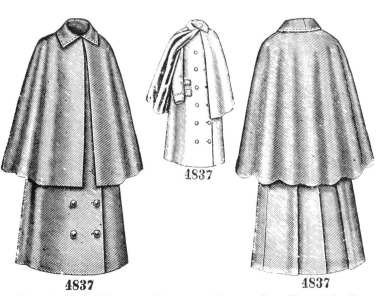

No. 4837.—GIRLS' COAT, WITH REMOVABLE MILITARY CAPE (Copyright).—The pattern of this coat is in 7 sizes for girls from 3 to 9 years of age, and may be developed in any seasonable coating. For a girl of 8 years, it requires 6⅛ yards of material 22 inches wide, or 3⅛ yards 44 inches wide, or 2⅝ yards 54 inches wide, with 2⅝ yards of silk 20 inches wide to line the cape. Price of pattern, 1s. or 25 cts.

No. 4741.—LADIES' WRAP (Copyright).—By referring to figure No. 407 A on page 95, another view of this comfortable garment may be seen. Plain cloth was chosen for the wrap in the present instance, and Astrakhan trims it handsomely. Bedford cord, chevron, diagonal serge, etc., may develop the mode, and passementerie, jet or any simple garniture may be added, with attractive results. The pattern is in 10 sizes for ladies from 28 to 46 inches, bust measure. For a lady of medium size, the wrap calls for 9⅜ yards of material 22 inches wide, or 4¾ yards 44 inches wide, or 4 yards 54 inches wide. Price of pattern, 1s. 6d. or 35 cents.

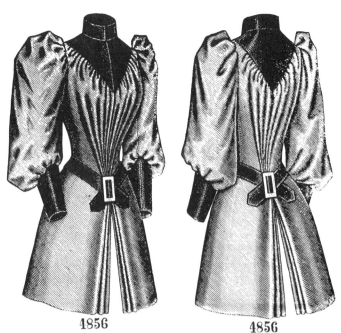

4856   **4856**

NO. 4856.—LADIES' BASQUE, WITH ATTACHED CIRCULAR SKIRT (Copyright).—This basque may be again seen by referring to figure No. 485 A on page 103 of this publication. The pattern is in 13 sizes for ladies from 28 to 46 inches, bust measure. To make the basque for a lady of medium size, will require 3 yards of dress goods 40 inches wide, with 1½ yard of velvet 20 inches wide. Of one material, it needs 6 yards 22 inches wide, or 3¼ yards 44 inches wide, or 3 yards 50 inches wide. Price of pattern, 1s. 3d. or 30 cents.

4774   **4774**

NO. 4774.—LADIES' LONG COAT (Copyright).—Fancy coating was used in the construction of this comfortable coat, and machine-stitching furnishes an appropriate finish. All kinds of coatings will make up in this fashion, and fur or a braid design may be applied for decoration. A plain completion is also suitable. The pattern is in 13 sizes for ladies from 28 to 46 inches, bust measure. To make the garment for a lady of medium size, will require 9¼ yards of goods 22 inches wide, or 7¼ yards 30 inches wide, or 4¾ yards 44 inches wide, or 4⅛ yards 54 inches wide. Price of pattern, 1s. 8d. or 40 cts.

FIGURE NO. 489 A.—MISSES' DRESS. —This illustrates Misses' dress No. 4818 (copyright), also shown on page 110. The pattern is in 7 sizes for misses from 10 to 16 years of age, and costs 1s. 3d. or 30 cents. In the combination pictured on page 110 for a miss of 12 years, the dress requires 3¾ yards of dress goods 40 inches wide, with 1⅜ yard of silk. Of one material, it calls for 6¾ yards 22 inches wide, or 3½ yards 44 inches wide.

FIGURE NO. 490 A.—MISSES' DRESS. —This represents Misses' dress No. 4845 (copyright), which is shown again on page 108 of the present issue. The pattern is in 7 sizes for misses from 10 to 16 years old, and costs 1s. 3d. or 30 cents. Of one material for a miss of 12 years, the dress calls for 7⅞ yards 22 inches wide, or 4 yards 44 inches wide, or 3½ yards 50 inches wide.

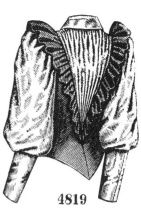

No. 4819.—
Misses' Basque
(Copyright). — At
figure No. 491 A
on this page this
basque is again
shown. The pattern is in 7 sizes
for misses from 10
to 16 years of age.
In the combination shown for a
miss of 12 years,
it requires 1
yard of dress
goods 40 inches
wide, with 2⅝
yard of silk. Price,
1s. or 25 cents.

4819

4819

Figure No. 491 A.—Misses' Basque.—This illustrates
Misses' basque No. 4819 (copyright), which is shown
again on this page. The pattern is in 7 sizes for misses
from 10 to 16 years of age, and costs 1s. or 25 cents. Of
one material for a miss of 12 years, it requires 4¼ yards
22 inches wide, or 2¼ yards 44 inches wide. As pictured elsewhere on this page, it needs 1 yard of dress
goods 40 inches wide, with 2⅝ yard of silk 20 ins. wide.

4838

4839   **4839**

No. 4839.—Girls' Apron (Copyright).—Fine
white cambric was chosen for making the apron
here shown, and edging and insertion supply the
decoration. The pattern is in 11 sizes for girls
from 2 to 12 years of age. To make the apron
for a girl of 8 years, needs 2⅝ yards of goods 36
inches wide. Price of pattern, 10d. or 20 cents.

4838

No. 4838.—Girls' Dress
(To be Worn with a
Guimpe) (Copyright).—This
pattern is in 8 sizes for girls,
from 5 to 12 years old. In,
the combination shown for a
girl of 8 years, it requires
3½ yards of figured challis
30 inches wide, and ¼ yard
of plain velvet 20 inches
wide. Of one material, it
needs 5 yards 22 inches wide,
or 2⅝ yards 44 inches wide,
or 2¼ yards 50 inches wide.
Price of pattern, 1s. or 25 cts.

Figure No. 469 A.—Ladies' Costume.—This illustrates
Ladies' costume No. 4852 (copyright), which is depicted
differently developed on page 107. The pattern is in 13
sizes for ladies from 28 to 46 inches, bust measure, and
costs 1s. 8d. or 40 cents. To make the costume for a lady
of medium size, will call for 9 yards of material 22 inches
wide, or 5⅛ yards 44 inches wide. If goods 50 inches
be chosen, then 4⅜ yards will be sufficient for the purpose.

99

4828

4828

FIGURE NO. 508 A.—LIT-
TLE GIRLS' SMOCKED DRESS.
— This illustrates Little
Girls' dress No. 4814 (copyright), which is also shown
on page 107. The pat-
tern is in 9 sizes for little
girls from ½ to 8 years old,
and costs 10d. or 20 cents.
For a girl of 5 years, the
dress will require 4¾ yards
of material 22 inches wide,
or 2⅜ yards 44 inches wide.

NO. 4828.—GIRLS' SMOCKED DRESS (Copyright).—
This pattern is in 8 sizes for girls from 5 to 12
years of age. As shown for a girl of 8 years, it
needs 2⅝ yards of dress goods 40 inches wide,
with 1⅛ yard of silk 20 inches wide. Of one material, it requires 5½ yards 22 inches wide, or 2¾
yards 44 ins. wide. Price of pattern, 1s. or 25 cts.

4809

4800

4797

NO. 4797.—MISSES' DRESS
(ALSO KNOWN AS THE PINA-
FORE DRESS) (Copyright).—This pattern is in 9 sizes for misses from 8 to
16 years of age. As illustrated for a miss of 12 years, it needs 3½ yards
of dress goods 40 inches wide, with ¾ yard of velvet 20 inches wide. Of
one material, it calls for 8⅛ yards 22 inches wide, or 5⅙ yards 30 inches
wide, or 3⅜ yards 44 inches wide. Price of pattern, 1s. 3d. or 30 cents.

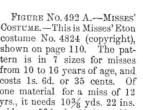

4797

NO. 4809. — LADIES' RUS-
SIAN-BLOUSE OVER-DRESS,
WITH WATTEAU BACK (Copy-
right).—The pattern of this
over-dress is in 13 sizes for
ladies from 28 to 46 inches,
bust measure. For a lady of
medium size, it needs 7¾ yards
of goods 22 inches wide, or 4⅝
yards 44 inches wide, or 3⅞
yards 50 inches wide. Price
of pattern, 1s. 6d. or 35 cents.

FIGURE NO. 492 A.—MISSES'
COSTUME.—This is Misses' Eton
costume No. 4824 (copyright),
shown on page 110. The pattern is in 7 sizes for misses
from 10 to 16 years of age, and
costs 1s. 6d. or 35 cents. Of
one material for a miss of 12
yrs., it needs 10⅜ yds. 22 ins.
wide, or 5⅜ yds. 44 ins. wide, or 4⅝ yds. 50 ins. wide. In the combination
shown on page 110, it needs 4⅛ yards of serge 40 ins. wide, and 4 yds. of silk.

4842   **4842**

No. 4842.—CHILD'S COAT (Copyright).—Bengaline was chosen for this dainty little topgarment, with fur and lace edging for garniture. The pattern is in 7 sizes for children from $\frac{1}{2}$ to 6 years of age, and will develop charmingly in faille, Bedford cord or smooth or rough surfaced cloth. For a child of 5 years, the coat requires $5\frac{1}{8}$ yards of material 22 inches wide, or $2\frac{1}{8}$ yards 44 inches wide, or $2\frac{1}{8}$ yards 54 inches wide. Price of pattern, 10d. or 20 cents.

4810   **4810**

No. 4810.—GIRLS' DRESS (Copyright).—A dainty combination of gray dress goods and gray silk is effected in this dress. It will develop nicely in all soft silks and woollens. Applied garniture is unnecessary, the shirrings providing the decoration. The pattern is in 8 sizes for girls from 5 to 12 years of age. As shown for a girl of 8 years, it requires $2\frac{5}{8}$ yards of dress goods 40 inches wide, with $1\frac{1}{2}$ yard of silk. Of one material, the dress requires $6\frac{1}{8}$ yards 22 inches wide, or $3\frac{1}{8}$ yards 44 inches wide. Price of pattern, 1s. or 25 cts.

FIGURE NO. 494 A.—MISSES' COSTUME.—This portrays Misses' costume No. 4807 (copyright), shown on page 107. The pattern is in 7 sizes for misses from 10 to 16 years of age, and costs 1s. 6d. or 35 cents. Of one material for a miss of 12 years, it requires $7\frac{3}{8}$ yards 22 inches wide, or $3\frac{5}{8}$ yards 44 ins. wide, or $3\frac{1}{8}$ yards 50 ins. wide.

1758

1758

1758   **1758**

No. 4758.—LADIES' RUSSIAN CLOAK (TO BE MADE WITHOUT CAPES OR WITH ONE, TWO OR THREE CAPES) (Copyright).—This cloak, which completely envelops the figure, is again portrayed at figure No. 427 A on page 99. It is here pictured developed in tan cloth, with bindings of fur for decoration. If desired, a perfectly plain finish may be adopted. The pattern is in 10 sizes for ladies from 28 to 46 inches, bust measure. For a lady of medium size, it requires 7 yards of material 36 inches wide, or 6 yards 44 inches wide, or 5 yards 54 inches wide. Price of pattern, 1s. 8d. or 40 cents.

No. 4835.—Misses' Coat, with Removable Military Cape (Copyright).—This stylish coat, which combines both utility and elegance, is represented developed in fancy coating and finished with machine-stitching. Storm serge, melton, cheviot and repellant cloth will make up nicely by the mode, and a plain finish will usually be adopted. The pattern is in 7 sizes for misses from 10 to 16 years old. For a miss of 12 years, it needs 8 yards of goods 22 inches wide, or 4⅛ yards 44 inches wide, or 3⅜ yards 54 inches wide. Price of pattern, 1s. 6d. or 35 cents.

No. 4813.—Little Girls' Dress (Copyright). — The pattern of this quaint dress is in 7 sizes for little girls from 2 to 8 years of age. To make the dress for a girl of 5 years, requires 4¾ yards of goods 22 inches wide. If material 44 inches wide be selected, then 2⅜ yards will suffice. Price of pattern, 10d. or 20 cents.

No. 4811.—Little Girls' Watteau Coat (Copyright). — This pattern is in 8 sizes for little girls from ½ to 7 years old. To make the coat for a girl of 5 years, will need 4⅜ yards of material 22 inches wide, or 2⅛ yards 44 inches wide, or 1¾ yard 54 inches wide. Price of pattern, 10d. or 20 cents.

Figure No. 463 A.—Ladies' Outdoor Toilette.—This consists of Ladies' wrap No. 4825 (copyr't), seen on page 110; and skirt No. 4833 (copyr't), on page 109. The wrap pattern is in 10 sizes for ladies from 28 to 46 ins., bust meas. The skirt pattern is in 9 sizes for ladies from 20 to 36 ins., waist meas. For prices, etc., see pages 109 and 110.

4847

4847

4847

No. 4847.—LA-DIES' LONG WRAP, PERFORATED FOR ROUND LENGTH (Copyr't). — This stylish wrap is also shown at figure No. 464 A on this page. It may be made with or without the cape, and may be made with a train as shown in the small engraving, or cut off in round length. The pattern is in 10 sizes for ladies from 28 to 46 inches, bust measure. In the combination shown for a lady of medium size, it will require 4⅞ yards of cloth 54 inches wide, with 2½ yards of lace flouncing 14½ inches wide, and ¾ yard of silk 20 inches wide. Of one material, it calls for 12¼ yards 22 inches wide, or 6 yards 44 inches wide or 5⅝ yards 54 inches wide. Price of pattern, 1s. 8d. or 40 cents.

4843

4843

No. 4843.— CHILD'S DRESS (Copyright).— The pattern of this graceful dress is in 6 sizes for children from 1 to 6 years of age. To make the garment for a child of 5 years, will require 5⅛ yards of goods 22 inches wide, or 4 yards 30 inches wide, or 2⅝ yards 44 inches wide. Price of pattern, 10d. or 20 cents.

No. 4799.—SOILED-CLOTHES BAG (Copyright).—This ornamental and useful bag is shown made of figured crêtonne and lined with Silesia. The pattern is in one size only, and, to make a bag like it, will require 3½ yards of goods 22 inches wide, or 2½ yards 27 inches or more in width, with 2½ yards of material 27 inches or more wide to line. Price of pattern, 5d. or 10 cents.

4799

FIGURE NO. 464 A.—LADIES' OUTDOOR TOILETTE.—This consists of La-dies' wrap No. 4847 (copyright), shown on this page; and skirt No. 4826 (copyr't), on page 110. The wrap pattern is in 10 sizes for ladies from 28 to 46 inches, bust measure. The skirt pattern is in 9 sizes for ladies from 20 to 36 inches, waist measure. For quantities, prices, etc., see pages 106 and 110.

SET NO. 152.—LADY DOLLS' ETON JACKET, CORNET SKIRT AND BLOUSE (Copyright).— This Set is also shown at figure No. 514 A on page 110 of this issue. It is in 7 sizes for lady dolls from 12 to 24 inches tall. For a doll 22 inches tall, the jacket and skirt require ⅞ yard of dress goods 40 inches wide, while the blouse needs 1⅛ yard of silk 20 inches wide. Price of Set, 10d. or 20 cents.

4853   **4853**

No. 4853.—LITTLE GIRLS' DRESS (Copyright).—This pattern is in 7 sizes for little girls from 2 to 8 years old. In the combination shown for a girl of 5 years, it requires 2¼ yards of cashmere 40 inches wide, with 2⅛ yards of silk. Of one material, it needs 5¼ yards 22 inches wide, or 2½ yards 44 inches wide. Price of pattern, 10d. or 20 cents.

4845   **4845**

4845

No. 4845.—MISSES' DRESS (Copyright).—This pattern, shown again at figure No. 490 A on page 104, is in 7 sizes for misses from 10 to 16 years of age. To make the dress for a miss of 12 years, calls for 7⅞ yards of goods 22 inches wide, or 4 yards 44 inches wide, or 3½ yards 50 inches wide. Price of pattern, 1s. 3d. or 30 cents.

FIGURE NO. 462 A.—LADIES' FULL-DRESS COSTUME.—This illustrates Ladies' full-dress costume No. 4848 (copyright), which is portrayed again elsewhere on this page. The pattern is in 13 sizes for ladies from 28 to 46 inches, bust measure, and costs 2s. or 50 cents. To make the costume of one material for a lady of medium size, will require 13½ yards 22 inches wide, or 7⅜ yards 44 inches wide, or 6¼ yards 50 inches wide. In the combination pictured elsewhere on this page, it requires 8⅝ yards of plain faille, with 5⅞ yards of brocaded silk 20 inches wide.

No. 4820. — LA-
DIES' SMOCKED
BLOUSE (WITH FIT-
TED LINING, WHICH
MAY BE OMITTED)
(Copyright). — T h i s
blouse is again shown
at figure No. 488 A on
page 103. It is here
depicted developed in
cream - white Surah.
All sorts of soft silken
and woollen fabrics
may be used for such
garments; and garni-
ture is omitted. The
pattern is in 13 sizes
for ladies from 28 to 46
inches, bust measure.
For a lady of medium
size, the blouse re-
quires 5⅝ yards of
goods 22 inches wide,
or 2⅞ yards 44 inch-
es wide. Price of pat-
tern, 1s. 3d. or 30 cts.

4820

4820

FIGURE NO.
513 A. — LADY
DOLLS' OUTDOOR
TOILETTE. — This
depicts the wrap
and skirt of Lady
Dolls' Set No. 153
(copyright).
which is fully
illustrated on
page 103. The
Set is in 7 sizes
for dolls from 12
to 24 inches tall,
and costs 10d.
or 20 cents. For
a doll 22 inches
tall, the skirt
and blouse will
require 1⅛ yard
of dress goods 40
inches wide;
while the wrap
needs ⅞ yard of
cloth 54 ins. wide.

FIGURE NO. 470 A — LADIES' COSTUME. — This represents
a partial front view of Ladies' costume No. 4852 (copyr't),
again pictured on this page. An entire back view is given
at figure No. 469 A on page 105. The pattern is in 13 sizes
for ladies from 28 to 46 inches, bust measure, and costs 1s. 8d.
or 40 cents. For a lady of medium size, it requires 9 yards
of material 22 inches wide, or 5⅛ yards 44 inches wide.

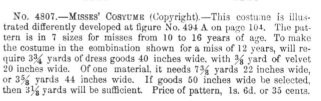

4807   **4807**

No. 4807. — MISSES' COSTUME (Copyright). — This costume is illustrated differently developed at figure No. 494 A on page 104. The pattern is in 7 sizes for misses from 10 to 16 years of age. To make
the costume in the combination shown for a miss of 12 years, will require 3¾ yards of dress goods 40 inches wide, with ⅜ yard of velvet
20 inches wide. Of one material, it needs 7⅜ yards 22 inches wide,
or 3⅝ yards 44 inches wide. If goods 50 inches wide be selected,
then 3⅛ yards will be sufficient. Price of pattern, 1s. 6d. or 35 cents.

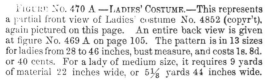

FIGURE NO. 516 A. — BOY DOLLS' SAILOR SUIT. — This portrays Boy
Dolls' Set No. 154 (copyright), shown on page 110. The suit will make
up nicely in flannel, serge, cheviot or cloth, and trimming may be sup-
plied by narrow braid or machine-stitching, or a plain finish be adopted. The Set is in
7 sizes for dolls from 12 to 24 inches tall. and costs 10d. or 20 cents. To make the Set for
a doll 22 inches tall, needs ¾ yard of white and ⅜ yard of blue flannel each 44 inches wide.

No. 4814. —
LITTLE GIRLS'
SMOCKED
DRESS (Copy-
right). — This
pattern, also
shown at fig-
ure No. 508 A
on page 105,
is in 9 sizes
for little girls
from ½ to 8
years of age.
For a girl of 5
years, it needs
4¾ yards of
goods 22 ins.
wide, or 2⅜
yards 44 ins.
wide. Price,
10d. or 20 cts.

4814   **4814**

4836　　　　　**4836**

No. 4836.—LADIES' COAT, WITH REMOVABLE MILITARY CAPE (Copyright).
—At figure No. 458 A on page 110 of this issue this coat is represented
made of plaid cheviot. It is here shown developed in fancy coating, machine-
stitching providing a neat finish. The pattern is in 13 sizes for ladies from
28 to 46 inches, bust measure. To make the garment for a lady of medium
size, requires 12½ yards of material 22 inches wide, or 6¼ yards 44 inches
wide, or 5⅜ yards 54 inches wide. Price of pattern, 1s. 8d. or 40 cents.

4821　　　　　**4821**

No. 4821.—GIRLS' DRESS (Copyright).—This pattern is in
8 sizes for girls from 5 to 12 years old. For a girl of 8
years. it requires 2¾ yards of dress goods 40 inches wide,
with ⅜ yard of velvet. Of one material, it needs 5½ yards
22 inches wide. Price of pattern, 1s. or 25 cents.

4806

4806　　　　　**4806**

No. 4806.—LADIES' ETON COSTUME, CONSISTING OF A SKIRT, VEST AND ETON
JACKET (Copyright).—This stylishly devised costume is again illustrated at figure
No. 474 A on page 109 of this publication. The above engravings picture it made
of dark serge and neatly finished with machine-stitching. The pattern is in 13
sizes for ladies from 28 to 46 inches, bust measure, and will develop stylishly in
cheviot, faced-cloth, cashmere, poplin, camel's-hair, vicuna or any other seasonable woollen fabric. To make the costume for a lady of medium size, will
require 10 yards of material 22 inches wide, or 4⅞ yards 44 inches wide. Of material 50 inches wide, 4¼ yards will be sufficient. Price of pattern, 1s. 8d. or 40 cents.

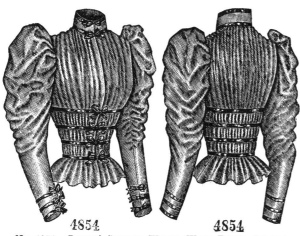

4854　　　　　**4854**

No. 4854.—LADIES' SHIRRED WAIST (WITH FITTED LINING)
(Copyright).—By referring to figure No. 461 A on page 103, another illustration of this waist may be seen. The pattern is in
11 sizes for ladies from 28 to 42 inches, bust measure. To
make the garment for a lady of medium size, needs 4¾ yards of
material 22 inches wide, or 2¾ yards 44 inches wide, or 2⅜
yards 50 inches wide. Price of pattern, 1s. or 25 cents.

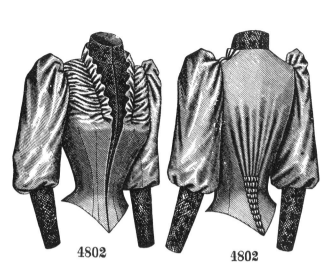

4802   4802

No. 4802.—LADIES' BASQUE (Copyright).—This pattern, seen at figure No. 487 A on page 103, is in 13 sizes for ladies from 28 to 46 inches, bust measure. For a lady of medium size. it needs 4⅛ yards of goods 22 inches wide, or 2¼ yards 44 inches wide, or 2 yards 50 inches wide. Price of pattern, 1s. 3d. or 30 cents.

4808   4808

No. 4808.—MISSES' PRINCESS WRAPPER (Copyright).— Dark cashmere was selected for the development of the wrapper shown in the accompanying engravings. The garment is notably simple in construction, and, although severe in effect, the addition of garniture, which may consist of lace ruffles, velvet, silk or ribbon, will render it very handsome. The pattern is in 9 sizes for misses from 8 to 16 years of age. To make the wrapper for a miss of 12 years, requires 6¾ yards of material 22 inches wide, or 5 yards 30 inches wide. Of goods 44 inches wide, 3¾ yards will be sufficient. Price of pattern. 1s. or 25 cents.

4852

4852   4852

No. 4852.—LADIES' COSTUME, WITH A SLIGHT TRAIN (PERFORATED FOR ROUND LENGTH) (Copyright).—By referring to figures Nos. 469 A on page 105 and 470 A elsewhere on this page, this costume may be seen differently developed. It is here pictured made of dress goods, and decoration is contributed by silk feather-trimming. The pattern is in 13 sizes for ladies from 28 to 46 inches, bust measure. To make the costume for a lady of medium size, will require 9 yards of material 22 inches wide, or 5⅛ yards 44 inches wide. Of goods 50 inches wide, 4⅜ yards will suffice. Price of pattern, 1s. 8d. or 40 cents.

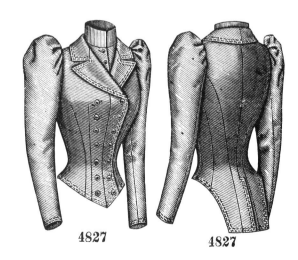

4827   4827

No. 4827.—LADIES' BASQUE (To BE MADE WITH OR WITHOUT A CHEMISETTE) (Copyright).—This pattern, shown at figure No. 479 A on page 109, is in 13 sizes for ladies from 28 to 46 inches. bust measure. For a lady of medium size. it needs 4⅝ yards of goods 22 ins. wide, or 2 yards 50 ins. wide. Price, 1s. 3d. or 30 cts.

4800

NO. 4800.— SHOE-AND-SLIPPER POCKET (Copyright).—This pattern is in one size, and, to make a pocket like it, will require ¾ yard of material 22 inches wide, or ⅝ yard 36 inches wide. Price of pattern, 5d. or 10 cents.

4848

NO. 4848.—LADIES' FULL–DRESS COSTUME, WITH ROUND TRAIN (PERFORATED FOR SLIGHTLY POINTED TRAIN) (Copyright).—At figure No. 462 A on this page this costume is shown developed in velvet and brocaded silk, with jet, lace and ostrich-feather band for decoration. The pattern is in 13 sizes for ladies from 28 to 46 inches, bust measure. In the combination shown for a lady of medium size, it needs 8⅝ yards of plain faille and 5⅞ yards of brocaded silk 20 inches wide. Of one material, it requires 13½ yards 22 inches wide, or 7¾ yards 44 inches wide, or 6¼ yards 50 inches wide. Price of pattern, 2s. or 50 cents.

4848

FIGURE NO. 509 A.—LITTLE GIRLS' DRESS.—This illustrates Little Girls' dress No. 4812 (copyright), differently represented on page 110 of this publication. The pattern is in 7 sizes for little girls from 1 to 7 years of age, and costs 10d. or 20 cents. To make the garment of one material for a girl of 5 years, will call for 4¾ yards 22 inches wide, or 2⅜ yards 44 inches wide, or 2 yards 50 inches wide.

4848

FIGURE NO. 460 A.—LADIES' PRINCESS CORSELET COSTUME.—This is Ladies' costume No. 4805 (copyright), again portrayed on page 108. The pattern is in 13 sizes for ladies from 28 to 46 inches, bust measure, and costs 1s. 8d. or 40 cents. For a lady of medium size, it needs 10¾ yards of goods 22 inches wide.

No. 4805.—LADIES' PRINCESS CORSELET COS-
TUME, WITH DEMI-TRAIN (PERFORATED FOR
ROUND LENGTH) (Copyright).—At figures Nos.
460 A and 486 A on pages 107 and 103 this costume is also shown. The pattern is in 13 sizes
for ladies from 28 to 46 inches, bust measure.
In the combination shown for a lady of medium
size, it requires 5⅝ yards of cashmere 40 inches
wide, with 1¾ yard of velvet 20 inches wide.
Of one material, it needs 10¾ yards 22 inches
wide, or 5⅝ yards 44 inches wide, or 5⅛ yards
50 inches wide. Price of pattern, 1s. 8d. or 40 cts.

4805

4805

4805

FIGURE NO. 564 A.—LITTLE
GIRLS' DRESS. — This portrays
Little Girls' dress No. 4911 (copyright), again pictured on page 115.
The pattern is in 8 sizes for little
girls from 2 to 9 years of age, and
costs 10d. or 20 cents. For a
girl of 5 years, it needs 4⅞ yards
of material 22 inches wide,
or 2½ yards 44 inches wide.

FIGURE NO. 514 A.—LA-
DY DOLLS' TOILETTE.—This
portrays Lady Dolls' Set
No. 152 (copyright), which
is also seen on page 107.
The Set is in 7 sizes for
dolls from 12 to 24 inches
tall, and costs 10d. or 20
cents. For a doll 22 inches
tall, the jacket and skirt call
for ⅞ yard of dress goods
40 inches wide; while the
blouse needs 1⅛ yard of silk.

FIGURE NO. 484 A.—LADIES' TOILETTE.—This consists of Ladies' basque
No. 4831 (copyright), shown on page 104; and skirt No. 4826 (copyright),
on page 110. The basque pattern is in 13 sizes for ladies from 28 to 46
inches, bust meas., and costs 1s. 3d. or 30 cents. The skirt pattern is in 9
sizes for ladies from 20 to 36 inches, waist meas., and costs 1s. 6d. or 35 cents.
For a lady of medium size, they need 6¾ yards of goods 44 inches wide.

4844

4844

No. 4844.—Girls' Dress (Copyright).— All sorts of fashionable materials will be chosen for developing the dress pictured in the accompanying engravings, and a combination of colors or fabrics may be introduced with effective results. The dress is illustrated made of old-rose cashmere, with réséda velvet ribbon for trimming. The pattern is in 8 sizes for girls from 5 to 12 years of age. To make the dress for a girl of 8 years, calls for 5⅜ yards of goods 22 inches wide, or 2⅝ yards 44 inches wide. Price of pattern, 1s. or 25 cents.

4840

4840

4840

No. 4840.—Ladies' Costume, with a Slight Train (Perforated for Round Length) (Copyright).—This pattern is in 13 sizes for ladies from 28 to 46 inches, bust measure. In the combination shown for a lady of medium size, it requires 5⅛ yards of dotted crépon 40 inches wide, with 2¾ yards of lace flouncing 11¼ inches wide. Of one material, it needs 10¾ yards 22 inches wide, or 5⅝ yards 44 inches wide, or 5 yards 50 inches wide. Price of pattern, 1s. 8d. or 40 cts.

Figure No. 474 A.—Ladies' Eton Costume.—This represents Ladies' Eton costume No. 4806 (copyr't), also portrayed on page 106. The pattern is in 13 sizes for ladies from 28 to 46 inches, bust measure, and costs 1s. 8d. or 40 cents. To make the costume for a lady of medium size, will require 10 yards of material 22 inches wide, or 4⅞ yards 44 inches wide, or 4¼ yards 50 inches wide.

No. 4841.—Misses' Long Basque (Copyright).—Woollen dress goods were selected for the construction of this basque, and fancy gimp decorates the collar and cuffs. The pattern is in 7 sizes for misses from 10 to 16 years of age. For a miss of 12 years, it requires 3¼ yards of material 22 inches wide, or 1⅝ yard 44 inches wide, or 1½ yard 50 inches wide. Price of pattern, 1s. or 25 cts.

4841

4841

4804

4804

4804

4804

Figure No. 479 A.—Ladies' Toilette.—This consists of Ladies' basque No. 4827 (copyright), shown on page 108; and skirt No. 4833 (copyr't), on this page. The basque pattern is in 13 sizes for ladies from 28 to 46 inches, bust measure, and costs 1s. 3d. or 30 cents. The skirt pattern is in 9 sizes for ladies from 20 to 36 inches, waist measure, and costs 1s. 6d. or 35 cts. For goods needed see pages 108 and 109.

No. 4804.—Ladies' Watteau Costume, with a Short Train (Perforated for Round Length) (Copyright).—This costume is again displayed at figure No. 471 A on page 104. The pattern is in 13 sizes for ladies from 28 to 46 inches, bust measure. For a lady of medium size, it requires 9⅜ yards of goods 22 inches wide, or 5 yards 44 inches wide, or 4⅛ yards 50 inches wide. Price of pattern, 1s. 8d. or 40 cts.

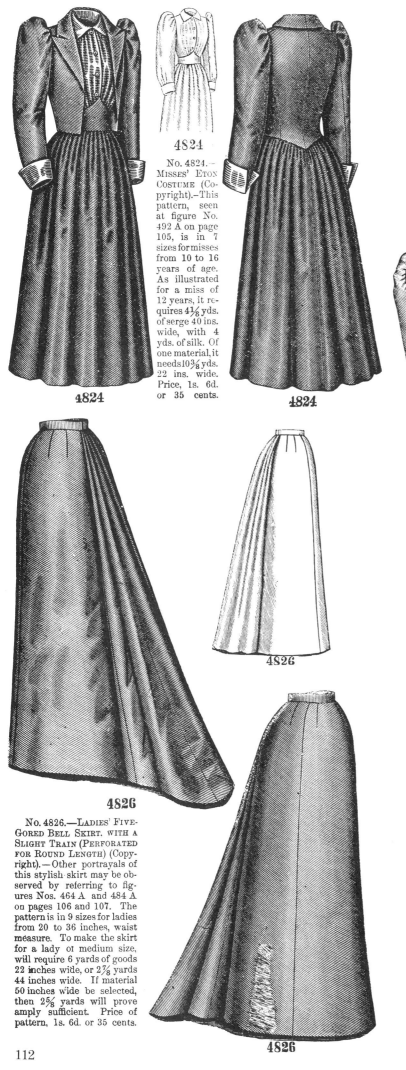

4824

No. 4824.—Misses' Eton Costume (Copyright).—This pattern, seen at figure No. 492 A on page 105, is in 7 sizes for misses from 10 to 16 years of age. As illustrated for a miss of 12 years, it requires 4⅛ yds. of serge 40 ins. wide, with 4 yds. of silk. Of one material, it needs 10⅜ yds. 22 ins. wide. Price, 1s. 6d. or 35 cents.

4824   **4824**

4826

4826

No. 4826.—Ladies' Five-Gored Bell Skirt. with a Slight Train (Perforated for Round Length) (Copyright).—Other portrayals of this stylish skirt may be observed by referring to figures Nos. 464 A and 484 A on pages 106 and 107. The pattern is in 9 sizes for ladies from 20 to 36 inches, waist measure. To make the skirt for a lady of medium size, will require 6 yards of goods 22 inches wide, or 2⅞ yards 44 inches wide. If material 50 inches wide be selected, then 2⅝ yards will prove amply sufficient. Price of pattern, 1s. 6d. or 35 cents.

4826

Set No. 154.—Boy Dolls' Sailor Trousers, Blouse and Cap (Copyr't).—This Set, shown at fig. No. 516 A on page 107, is in 7 sizes for dolls from 12 to 24 ins. tall. For a doll 22 ins. tall, it needs ¾ yard of white and ⅜ yard of blue flannel 44 ins. wide. Price, 10d. or 20 cts.

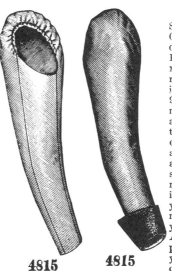

No. 4815. — Ladies' Sleeve (For Street Garments), with Round or Pointed Cuff, and Fitted Lining, Which may be Omitted (Copyright).—This pattern is in 7 sizes for ladies from 9 to 15 inches, arm measure, measuring the arm about an inch below the bottom of the arm's-eye. For a lady whose arm measures 11 inches as described, a pair of sleeves with round cuffs needs ⅞ yard of cloth 54 inches wide, with ⅜ yard of velvet. Of one material, it needs 1⅞ yard 22 inches wide. A pair of sleeves with pointed cuffs calls for 2 yards 22 ins. wide. Price of pattern, 5d. or 10 cts.

4815   **4815**   **4815**

4823   **4823**

No. 4823.—Misses' Costume (Copyright).—Silk and dress goods are combined in the stylish costume illustrated in the accompanying engravings. The pattern is in 7 sizes for misses from 10 to 16 years of age. To make the costume as represented for a miss of 12 years, will require 3⅞ yards of dress goods 40 inches wide, and 1⅜ yard of silk 20 inches wide. Of one material, it calls for 6¾ yards 22 inches wide, or 3½ yards 44 inches wide. If goods 50 inches wide be selected, then 2⅞ yards will prove sufficient. Price of pattern, 1s. 6d. or 35 cents.

No. 4812.— Little Girls' Dress (Copyr't). —This pattern, also shown at figure No. 509 A on page 108, is in 7 sizes for little girls from 1 to 7 years of age. To make the dress for a girl of 5 years, will require 4¾ yards of material 22 inches wide, or 2⅜ yards 44 inches wide, or 2 yards 50 inches wide. Price of pattern, 10d. or 20 cents.

4812

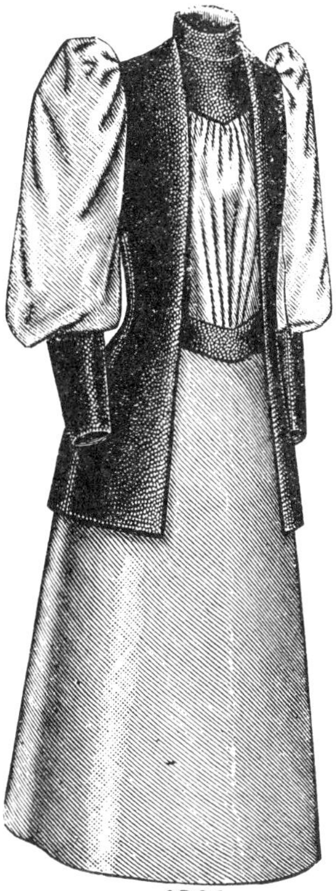

4812

No. 4801.— Misses' Costume (Copyright). — The pattern of this stylishly devised costume is in 7 sizes for misses from 10 to 16 years of age. To make the costume in the combination represented for a miss of 12 years, will require 2⅝ yards of dress goods 40 inches wide, with 2⅜ yards of velvet 20 inches wide. Of one material, it calls for 7⅛ yards 22 inches wide, or 3½ yards 44 inches wide. Price of pattern, 1s. 6d. or 35 cents.

4801

4801

No. 4876.— Ladies' Eton Basque (Copyright).—By referring to figure No. 535 A on page 111, this stylish basque may be again observed. The pattern is in 13 sizes for ladies from 28 to 46 inches. bust measure. For a lady of medium size, it needs 2¼ yards of dress goods 40 inches wide. and ⅝ yard of silk. Of one material, it will require 4¾ yards 22 inches wide, or 2⅜ yards 44 inches wide, or 2⅛ yards 50 inches wide. Price of pattern, 1s. 3d. or 30 cents.

4876

4876

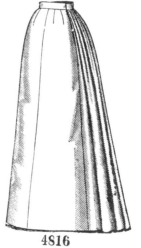

4816

4816

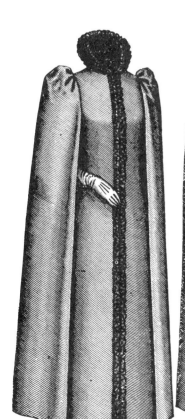

4834

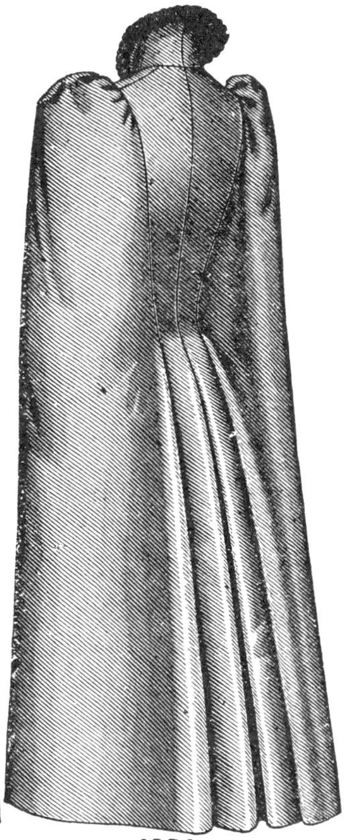

4834

No. 4834.— Misses' Russian Circular Wrap (Copyright).—An attractive combination of cloth and fur is pictured in this comfortable wrap. Cheviot, melton, kersey, beaver and, in fact, all varieties of seasonable coatings are adaptable to the mode, while mink, sable, beaver, monkey, Astrakhan or any fashionable fur will supply ample decoration. The pattern is in 7 sizes for misses from 10 to 16 years of age. For a miss of 12 years, it needs 2⅝ yards of cloth 54 inches wide, with a piece of Persian lamb measuring 9 x 10 inches. Of one material, it will require 6 yards 22 inches wide, or 3⅜ yards 44 inches wide, or 2⅝ yards 54 inches wide. Price of pattern, 1s. 6d. or 35 cents.

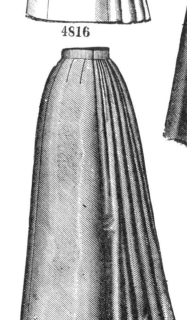

4816

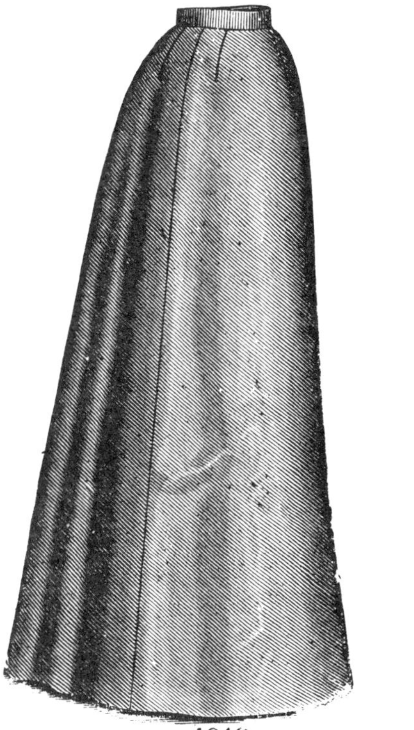

No. 4816.— Ladies' Four-Gored Skirt, with a Bell-Gored Foundation, and a Short Train (Perforated for Round Length) (Desirable for Stout Ladies) (Copyright). — Other views of this skirt are portrayed at figures Nos. 485 A, 456 A and 457 A on pages 103, 106 and 110. The pattern is in 11 sizes for ladies from 20 to 40 inches, waist measure. To make the skirt for a lady of medium size, will require 6⅜ yards of material 22 inches wide, or 3⅛ yards 44 inches wide, or 3⅛ yards 50 inches wide. Price of pattern, 1s. 6d. or 35 cents.

4818   **4818**

No. 4818.—Misses' Dress (Copyright).—This dress is differently illustrated at figure No. 489 A on page 104 of this publication. The pattern is in 7 sizes for misses from 10 to 16 years of age. To make the dress of one material for a miss of 12 years, will need 6¾ yards 22 inches wide, or 3½ yards 44 inches wide. In the combination here shown, it will require 3¾ yards of dress goods 40 inches wide, with 1⅜ yard of silk 20 inches wide. Price of pattern, 1s. 3d. or 30 cents.

Figure No. 457 A.—Ladies' Outdoor Toilette.—This consists of Ladies' coat No. 4849 (copyright), seen on page 103 ; and skirt No. 4816 (copyright), on page 109. The coat pattern is in 13 sizes for ladies from 28 to 46 inches, bust measure; the skirt pattern is in 11 sizes for ladies from 20 to 40 inches, waist measure, and each costs 1s. 6d. or 35 cents. For quantities of goods needed, see pages 103 and 109.

4825   **4825**   **4825**

No. 4825.—Ladies' Wrap (Copyright).—This stylish wrap is shown differently developed at figure No. 463 A on page 106. The pattern is in 10 sizes for ladies from 28 to 46 inches, bust measure. To make the wrap for a lady of medium size, will call for 3¼ yards of Sicilienne 36 inches wide, with 4½ yards of lace flouncing 13½ inches wide. Of one material, it needs 7¾ yards 22 inches wide, or 4 yards 44 inches wide, or 3½ yards 54 inches wide. Price of pattern, 1s. 6d. or 35 cents

4872

4872

No. 4872.—LADIES' JACKET (Copyright).—By referring to figure No. 548 A on page 114, this jacket may be again seen. Cloth was here used for the garment. All fashionable varieties of coatings, such as cheviot, melton, kersey or broadcloth, may be employed for making the jacket, and the decoration may be contributed by braid, passementerie or machine-stitching. The pattern is in 13 sizes for ladies from 28 to 46 inches, bust measure. For a lady of medium size, it requires 6¾ yards of material 22 inches wide, or 3⅜ yards 44 inches wide, or 2¾ yards 54 inches wide. Price of pattern, 1s. 6d. or 35 cents.

FIGURE NO. 456 A.—LADIES' OUTDOOR TOILETTE. —This consists of Ladies' coat No. 4855 (copyright), which is also represented on page 103; and skirt No. 4816 (copyright), shown on page 109. The coat pattern is in 13 sizes for ladies from 28 to 46 inches, bust measure, and costs 1s. 6d. or 35 cents. The skirt pattern is in 11 sizes for ladies from 20 to 40 inches, waist measure, and costs 1s. 6d. or 35 cents. Of goods 22 inches wide for a lady of medium size, the coat needs 6½ yards, and the skirt, 6⅜ yards.

4803

4803

4803

No. 4803.—DOMINO AND MASK (Copyright).—The engravings picture a domino and mask made of Silesia. The domino may be made with or without a train, and the sleeves may be gathered at the wrists or left to flow, as preferred. The mask reaches to the nose, and to the lower edge is joined a frill of lace. The pattern is in 5 sizes from 30 to 46 inches, chest measure. For a person of 34 inches, chest measure, the domino requires 12⅜ yards of material 22 inches wide, or 7⅜ yards 36 inches wide, or 6½ yards 44 inches wide. The mask needs ⅛ yard of silk 20 inches wide. Price of pattern, 1s. 8d. or 40 cts.

4894

4894

4894

NO. 4894.—LADIES' TRIPLE CIR-
CULAR CAPE (KNOWN AS THE
VICTORIA CAPE) (Copyright).—
This cape is shown again at figure
No. 542 A on page 113. It is here
pictured made of cloth and velvet.
The pattern is in 10 sizes for ladies
from 28 to 46 inches, bust measure. In the combination shown for
a lady of medium size, the cape
calls for 2⅜ yards of cloth 54
inches wide, and ⅝ yard of velvet
(cut bias) 20 inches wide. Of one
material, it needs 2⅞ yards 44
inches wide, or 2⅝ yards 54 inches
wide. Price of pattern, 1s. or 25 cts.

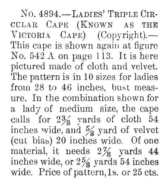

FIGURE No. 560 A.—GIRLS' TOIL-
ETTE.—This consists of Girls' blouse
dress No. 4891 (copyright), shown on
page 113; and guimpe No. 4888 (copyright), on page 112. The dress pattern is in 8 sizes for girls from 5 to
12 years old, and costs 1s. or 25 cts.
The guimpe pattern is in 13 sizes
from ½ to 12 years old, and costs
5d. or 10 cents. For a girl of 8
years, the dress needs 4¾ yards of
material 22 inches wide; the guimpe
needs 2 yards the same width.

FIGURE No. 561 A. — GIRLS'
DRESS. — This depicts Girls'
dress No. 4889 (copyright), again
illustrated on page 114. The pattern is in 8 sizes for girls from 5
to 12 years of age, and costs 1s.
or 25 cents. For a girl of 8 years,
it needs 5⅝ yards of goods 22 inches wide. or 4⅜ yards 30 inches
wide, or 3 yards 44 inches wide.

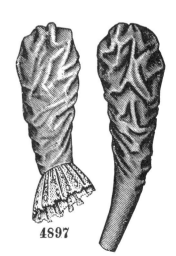

4897

4897

NO. 4897.—LADIES' WRINKLED DRESS SLEEVE
(Copyright).—This pattern is in 7 sizes for ladies
from 9 to 15 inches, arm measure, measuring the
arm about an inch below the bottom of the arm's-
eye. For a lady whose arm measures 11 inches
as described, a pair of long sleeeves needs 1⅝ yard
of goods 22 inches wide, or 1⅛ yard 44 inches
wide, or ⅞ yard 50 inches wide. A pair of elbow
sleeves needs 1⅜ yard 22 inches wide, or ¾ yard
44 or 50 inches wide. Price of pattern, 5d. or 10 cts.

FIGURE No. 538 A.—LADIES' EVENING WAIST.—This represents Ladies' waist No. 4880 (copyright), which is again shown
on page 112 of this publication. The pattern is in 13 sizes for
ladies from 28 to 46 inches, bust measure, and costs 1s. or
25 cents. To make the waist with flounce sleeves for a lady
of medium size, will require 3½ yards of material 22 inches
wide, or 3 yards 27 inches wide, or 2 yards 44 inches
wide. The waist with puff sleeves needs 4 yards 22 inches
wide, or 3¼ yards 27 inches wide, or 2¼ yards 44 inches wide.

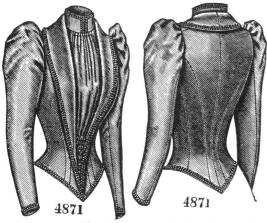

4871   **4871**

No. 4871.—Ladies' Basque (Copyright).—This stylishly designed basque is again shown at figure No. 539 A on this page. The pattern is in 13 sizes for ladies from 28 to 46 inches, bust measure. To make the basque for a lady of medium size, will require 4⅜ yards of material 22 inches wide, or 2⅛ yards 44 inches wide. If goods 50 inches wide be chosen, 1⅞ yard will prove amply sufficient. Price of pattern, 1s. 3d. or 30 cts.

4858

No. 4858. — Dogs' Blanket (Copyright). — This blanket is shown made of chamois and trimmed with moss-trimming. The pattern is in 3 sizes for dogs measuring 8, 12 and 16 inches along the center of the back. For a dog measuring 12 inches, it requires a piece of chamois 17½ x 21 inches, or ⅞ yard of goods 20 inches wide, or ½ yard 27 inches or more wide. Price of pattern, 7d. or 15 cents.

Figure No. 535 A.—Ladies' Eton Basque.—This portrays Ladies' basque No. 4876 (copyright), shown again on page 118. The pattern is in 13 sizes for ladies from 28 to 46 inches, bust measure, and costs 1s. 3d. or 30 cents. For a lady of medium size, the basque requires 4¾ yards of material 22 inches wide, or 2⅜ yard 44 inches wide, or 2⅛ yards 50 inches wide. In the combination shown on page 118, it needs 2¼ yards of dress goods 40 inches wide, with ⅝ yard of silk.

Figure No. 562 A.—Little Girls' Dress.—This illustrates Little Girls' dress No. 4863 (copyright), which is again portrayed on page 115 of this issue. The pattern is in 7 sizes for little girls from ½ to 6 years of age, and costs 10d. or 20 cents. For a girl of 5 years, the dress needs 5 yards of material 22 inches wide, or 2½ yards 44 inches wide.

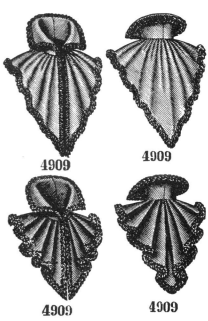

4909   **4909**

4909   **4909**

No. 4909.—Ladies' Collars (Known as the Derby Collars) (Copyright).—Cloth was chosen for making this cape, and feather trimming provides ample decoration. The pattern is in 3 sizes—small, medium and large. In the medium size, the collar with plaited cape calls for 1½ yard of goods 22 inches wide, or ⅞ yard 44 inches wide, or ⅝ yard 54 inches wide. The collar with gathered cape needs 1⅜ yard of goods 22 inches wide, or ¾ yard 44 inches wide, or ⅝ yard 54 inches wide. Price of pattern, 5d. or 10 cents.

Figure No. 539 A. — Ladies' Basque. — This illustrates Ladies' basque No. 4871 (copyright), which is again represented on this page. The pattern is in 13 sizes for ladies from 28 to 46 inches, bust measure, and costs 1s. 3d. or 30 cents. For a lady of medium size, it requires 4⅜ yards of goods 22 inches wide, or 2⅛ yards 44 inches wide, or 1⅞ yard 50 inches wide.

No. 4851.—Ladies' Wrapper (With Fitted Lining) (Copyright)—The pattern of this graceful wrapper is in 13 sizes for ladies from 28 to 46 inches, bust measure. To make the garment for a lady of medium size, calls for 11⅛ yards of material 22 inches wide, or 8 yards 30 inches wide, or 5⅞ yards 44 inches wide. Price of pattern, 1s. 6d. or 35 cents.

No. 4822.—Ladies' Wrapper, with Fitted Body-Lining, and a Slight Train (Perforated for Round Length) (Copyright).—This pattern is in 13 sizes for ladies from 28 to 46 inches, bust measure. For a lady of medium size, it requires 12 yards of material 22 inches wide, or 6⅜ yards 44 inches wide, or 5⅛ yards 50 ins. wide. Price of pattern, 1s. 6d. or 35 cts.

No. 4867 — Misses' Mother-Hubbard Wrapper, with Under-Arm Gore (Copyright).— Another view of this comfortably devised wrapper is given at figure No. 554 A on page 114 of this publication. Figured cashmere was chosen for the development of the garment in the present instance, and a perfectly plain finish is observable at all the edges. The pattern is in 7 sizes for misses from 10 to 16 years of age. To make the garment for a miss of 12 years, requires 6¾ yards of material 22 inches wide, or 4⅞ yards 30 inches wide. Of goods 44 inches wide, 3⅜ yards will be sufficient. Price of pattern, 1s. or 25 cents.

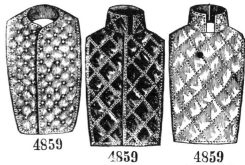

No. 4859.—Men's Chest-Shields (Copyright).— The pattern of these comfortable shields here pictured is in 3 sizes, 11, 13 and 15 inches long at the center of the front. In the medium size, the shield whole in the front will require ½ yard of material 20 inches wide; while the shield without a collar and the shield open in front and with a collar each calls for ⅝ yard 20 inches wide. Price of pattern, 7d. or 15 cents.

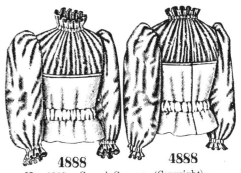

No. 4888.—Girls' Guimpe (Copyright).— At figure No. 560 A on page 111 of this issue, this guimpe may be again seen. The pattern is in 13 sizes for girls from ½ to 12 years of age. For a girl of 8 years, it requires 2 yards of material 22 inches wide, or 1⅜ yard 36 inches wide, or 1 yard 44 inches wide. Price of pattern, 5d. or 10 cents.

4829

4829

4829

NO. 4829.—LADIES' PRINCESS COSTUME, WITH CORNET BACK, AND A SLIGHT TRAIN (PERFORATED FOR ROUND LENGTH) (Copyright).—This costume is also shown at figure No. 468 A on page 103. Figured silk and plain dress goods are here united. The pattern is in 13 sizes for ladies from 28 to 46 inches, bust measure. For a lady of medium size, it requires 5⅝ yards of plain dress goods 40 inches wide, with 4 yards of figured silk. Of one material, it needs 11½ yards 22 inches wide, or 6⅛ yards 44 inches wide, or 5⅜ yards 50 inches wide. Price of pattern, 1s. 8d. or 40 cents.

4869

4869

4869

4869

4869

No. 4869.—LADIES' CAPE (KNOWN AS THE DERBY CAPE) (Copyright).—By referring to figure No. 545 A on page 118 of this publication, another view of this cape may be observed. The pattern is in 10 sizes for ladies from 28 to 46 inches, bust measure. To make the cape of one material for a lady of medium size, requires 2 yards either 44, 50 or 54 inches wide. Price of pattern, 10d. or 20 cts.

4904

4904

No. 4904.—MISSES' RUSSIAN COAT (Copyright).—A different portrayal of this coat is given at figure No. 550 A on page 116 of this publication. The pattern is in 7 sizes for misses from 10 to 16 years of age. For a miss of 12 years, it will require 4⅞ yards of material 22 inches wide, or 2¾ yards 44 inches wide, or 2⅛ yards 54 inches wide. Price of pattern, 1s. 3d. or 30 cents.

4901

4901

No. 4901.—LADIES' FANCY APRON (Copyright).—This charming apron is pictured made of nainsook, and prettily decorated with embroidery and drawn-work. The pattern is in 4 sizes for ladies from 20 to 32 inches, waist measure. For a lady of medium size, it will require 2⅝ yards of material 22 inches wide, or 2⅛ yards 36 inches wide. Price of pattern, 7d. or 15 cents.

119

SET NO. 156.—GIRL DOLLS' DRESS, COMMODORE JACKET AND CAP (Copyright).—This Set, shown again at figure No. 571 A on page 114, is in 7 sizes for dolls from 12 to 24 inches tall. For a doll 22 inches tall, the dress will require $\frac{5}{8}$ yard of cashmere 40 inches wide, with $\frac{5}{8}$ yard of silk 20 inches wide; while the cap and jacket need $\frac{1}{2}$ yard of cloth 54 inches wide. Price of Set, 10d. or 20 cents.

FIGURE NO. 567 A.—INFANTS' SLIP.—This depicts Infants' slip No. 4902 (copyright), shown again on page 115. The pattern is in one size, and costs 7d. or 15 cents. To make a slip like it, requires $2\frac{1}{4}$ yards of any appropriate material 36 inches wide.

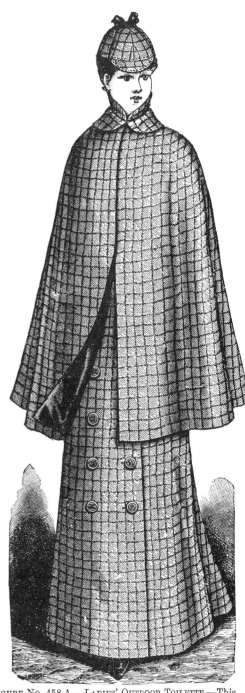

FIGURE NO. 458 A.—LADIES' OUTDOOR TOILETTE.—This consists of Ladies' coat No. 4836 (copyright), seen on page 107; and cap No. 2175, on page 14. The coat pattern is in 13 sizes for ladies from 28 to 46 inches, bust measure, and costs 1s. 8d. or 40 cents. The cap pattern is in 7 sizes from 6 to $7\frac{1}{2}$, hat sizes, or from $19\frac{1}{4}$ to $23\frac{3}{4}$ inches, head measures, and costs 5d. or 10 cents. For a lady of medium size, they need $6\frac{5}{8}$ yards of goods 44 inches wide.

FIGURE NO. 542 A.—LADIES' VICTORIA CAPE.—This pictures Ladies' cape No. 4894 (copyright), shown on page 111. The pattern is in 10 sizes for ladies from 28 to 46 inches, bust measure, and costs 1s. or 25 cents. Of one material for a lady of medium size, it needs $2\frac{7}{8}$ yards 44 inches wide, or $2\frac{5}{8}$ yards 54 inches wide.

FIGURE NO. 541 A.—LADIES' BASQUE.—This is Ladies'
basque No. 4892 (copyright), also shown on page 114.
The pattern is in 13 sizes for ladies from 28 to 46 inches, bust measure, and costs 1s. 3d. or 30 cents. In the
combination shown on page 114 for a lady of medium size,
it calls for $2\frac{3}{8}$ yards of dress goods 40 inches wide, with
$2\frac{7}{8}$ yards of silk 20 inches wide. Of one material, it
needs 6 yds. 22 inches wide, or $3\frac{1}{4}$ yards 44 inches wide.

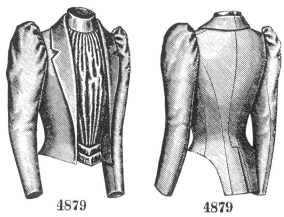

4879   **4879**

NO. 4879. — MISSES' COAT-BASQUE, WITH ETON JACKET-
FRONTS (ALSO KNOWN AS THE MARLOW BASQUE) (Copyright).—
This pattern, again displayed at figure No. 553 A on page 118,
is in 7 sizes for misses from 10 to 16 years of age. As
represented for a miss of 12 years, the garment needs $1\frac{3}{8}$
yard of serge 44 inches wide, with 1 yard of silk 20 inches
wide. Of one material, it requires $3\frac{5}{8}$ yards 22 inches wide,
or $1\frac{7}{8}$ yard 44 inches wide. Price of pattern, 1s. or 25 cents.

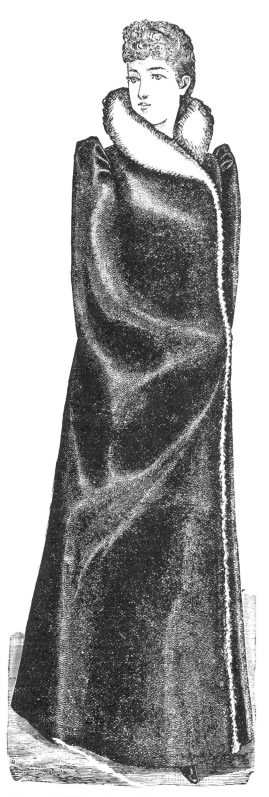

FIGURE NO. 531 A.—LADIES' RUSSIAN WRAP.—This represents Ladies' wrap No. 4895 (copyright). The pattern is
in 10 sizes for ladies from 28 to 46 inches, bust measure, and
costs 1s. 8d. or 40 cents. For a lady of medium size, the wrap
needs $5\frac{1}{8}$ yards of material 36 or 44 inches wide, or $3\frac{1}{2}$
yards 54 inches wide.

4887

4868

4887

No. 4887.—Ladies' Empire Costume, with a Slight Train (Perforated for Round Length) (Copyright).—This pattern, also shown at figures Nos. 528 A and 527 A on pages 116 and 117, is in 13 sizes for ladies from 28 to 46 inches, bust measure. In the combination shown for a lady of medium size, it needs 5 yards of dress goods 40 inches wide, with 1¾ yard of velvet and 2½ yards of silk 20 inches wide. Price of pattern, 1s. 8d. or 40 cents.

4908   4908

4908

No. 4908. — Misses' and Girls' Triple Circular Cape (Known as the Victoria Cape) (Copyright).—At figure No. 556 A on page 116 this cape is shown differently developed. The pattern is in 7 sizes from 4 to 16 years of age. In the combination shown for a miss of 12 years, it needs 2¼ yards of cloth 54 inches wide, and ½ yard of velvet (cut bias) 20 inches wide. Of one material, it requires 2½ yards 44 inches wide, or 2⅜ yards 54 ins. wide. Price of pattern, 10d. or 20 cts.

4908

No. 4868.—Ladies' Russian Wrap (Copyright). — This wrap is illustrated made of cloth and Persian lamb. The pattern is in 10 sizes for ladies from 28 to 46 inches, bust measure. In the combination pictured for a lady of medium size, it needs 4¼ yards of cloth 54 inches wide, with a piece of Persian lamb measuring 10¼x11 inches. Of one material, it calls for 5 yards 36 inches wide, or 4⅞ yards 44 inches wide, or 4¼ yards 54 ins. de. Price of pattern, 1s. 8d. or 40 cents.

4868

4864

4912

4912

4912

No. 4912.—Ladies' Short-Waist Empire Gown, with Fitted Body-Lining, and a Short Train (Perforated for Round Skirt and Square, Round and Pointed Neck) (Copyright).—This pattern, also shown at figure No. 532 A on page 117, is in 13 sizes for ladies from 28 to 46 inches, bust measure. Of one material for a lady of medium size, it requires 10½ yards 22 inches wide, or 8½ yards 27 inches wide, or 5⅞ yards 44 inches wide. Price of pattern, 1s. 6d. or 35 cents.

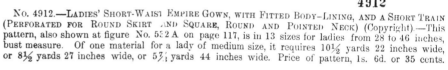

1880

4880

No. 4880. — Ladies' Evening Waist (Copyr't). —This pattern, shown on page 111 at figure No. 538 A is in 13 sizes for ladies from 28 to 46 inches, bust measure. For a lady of medium size, the waist with puff sleeves needs 2⅝ yds. of *crêpe de Chine* 27 inches wide, with 3⅝ yds. of lace edging 6 ins. wide. The waist with flounce sleeves needs 1⅞ yard of *crêpe de Chine*, with 3⅝ yards of lace edging, and 1⅜ yd. of lace flouncing 11 ins. wide. Price, 1s. or 25 cts.

4864

No. 4864.—Ladies' Cloak (Copyright).—This handsome cloak is pictured made of cloth and richly trimmed with passementerie. Fancy and plain cloakings are popular for cloaks of this kind, and fur or braiding are suitable garnitures. The pattern is in 10 sizes for ladies from 28 to 46 inches, bust measure. To make the garment for a lady of medium size, requires 6 yards of material 36 inches wide, or 4¾ yards 44 inches wide. If goods 54 inches wide be chosen, 3⅝ yards will suffice. Price of pattern, 1s. 8d. or 40 cents.

No. 4891.—Girls' Blouse Dress (To be Worn with a Guimpe) (Copyright).—This dress is again depicted at figure No. 560 A on page 111. The pattern is in 8 sizes for girls from 5 to 12 years of age. To make the garment for a girl of 8 years, needs 4¾ yards of goods 22 inches wide, or 3½ yards 30 inches wide, or 2⅜ yards 44 inches wide. Price of pattern, 1s. or 25 cents.

4891

4891

4862

4862

4862

No. 4862.—Ladies' Coat. (For Wear With or Without Cape-Collars) (Copyright).—This coat is again depicted at figure No. 523 A on page 117. The pattern is in 13 sizes for ladies from 28 to 46 inches, bust measure. To make the coat of one material for a lady of medium size, will require 9⅛ yards 22 inches wide, or 4½ yards 44 inches wide, or 3⅞ yards 54 inches wide. Price of pattern, 1s. 6d. or 35 cents.

Figure No. 557 A.—Girls' Russian Coat.—This illustrates Girls' coat No. 4900 (copyright), shown differently developed on page 116. Smooth coating and velvet are here artistically united in the coat. The pattern is in 8 sizes for girls from 5 to 12 years of age, and costs 1s. or 25 cents. Of one material for a girl of 8 years, it calls for 4¾ yards 22 inches wide, or 2¾ yards 44 inches wide, or 2¼ yards 54 inches wide.

4895

4895

4895

4895

No. 4895.—Ladies' Russian Wrap (Copyright).—This stylish garment is illustrated differently made up at figure No. 531 A on page 113. It is here shown made of cloth, with fur for decoration. The center seam may be closed to the lower edge or terminated a little below the waist-line, as preferred. The pattern is in 10 sizes for ladies from 28 to 46 inches, bust measure. For a lady of medium size, it will require 5⅛ yards of goods 36 or 44 inches wide, or 3½ yards 54 inches wide. Price of pattern, 1s. 8d. or 40 cents.

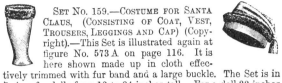
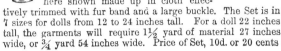

SET No. 159.—COSTUME FOR SANTA CLAUS, (CONSISTING OF COAT, VEST, TROUSERS, LEGGINGS AND CAP) (Copyright).—This Set is illustrated again at figure No. 573 A on page 116. It is here shown made up in cloth effectively trimmed with fur band and a large buckle. The Set is in 7 sizes for dolls from 12 to 24 inches tall. For a doll 22 inches tall, the garments will require 1½ yard of material 27 inches wide, or ¾ yard 54 inches wide. Price of Set, 10d. or 20 cents

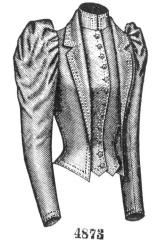
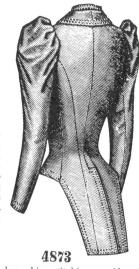
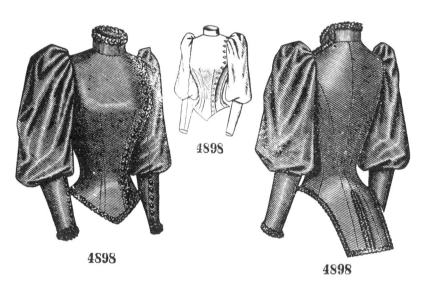

4873

No. 4873.—LADIES' COAT-BASQUE, WITH ETON JACKET-FRONTS (ALSO KNOWN AS THE MARLOW BASQUE) (Copyright). — At figure No. 530 A on page 118 this basque is again portrayed. Diagonal serge was here chosen for the development of the basque, and machine-stitching provides a neat finish. The pattern is in 13 sizes for ladies from 28 to 46 inches, bust measure. To make the basque for a lady of medium size, will require 4¾ yards of material 22 inches wide, or 2⅜ yards 44 inches wide. If 50-inch-wide goods be selected, 2¼ yards will suffice. Price of pattern, 1s. 3d. or 30 cents.

FIGURE No. 554 A.—MISSES' MOTHER-HUBBARD WRAPPER.—This illustrates Misses' wrapper No. 4867 (copyright), again pictured on page 112. In this instance pink cashmere embroidered with white dots is represented in the dress, with pink satin-edged ribbon for garniture. All woollen textures will make up nicely in this way, and less expensive cotton goods will also be used. The pattern is in 7 sizes for misses from 10 to 16 years of age, and costs 1s. or 25 cents. To make the garment for a miss of 12 years, requires 6¾ yards of material 22 inches wide, or 4⅞ yards 30 inches wide, or 3⅜ yards 44 inches wide.

4898

4898   4898

No. 4898.—LADIES' BASQUE (Copyright).—This modish basque is again represented at figure No. 520 A on page 117. Dark-green cloth was here chosen for its construction, and Astrakhan bindings and buttons furnish the completion. The pattern is in 13 sizes for ladies from 28 to 46 inches, bust measure. To make the basque for a lady of medium size, needs 4 yards of goods 22 inches wide, or 2 yards 44 inches wide, or 1⅞ yard 50 inches wide. Price of pattern, 1s. 3d. or 30 cts.

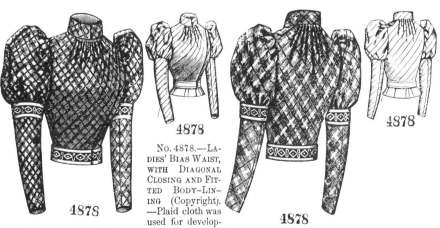

4878

4878   4878

No. 4878.—LADIES' BIAS WAIST, WITH DIAGONAL CLOSING AND FITTED BODY-LINING (Copyright). —Plaid cloth was used for developing this pretty waist, and passementerie provides the simple decoration. The pattern is in 13 sizes for ladies from 28 to 46 inches, bust measure. To make the garment for a lady of medium size, requires 3½ yards of goods 22 inches wide, or 2⅛ yards 44 inches wide, or 1¾ yard 50 inches wide. Price of pattern, 1s. or 25 cents.

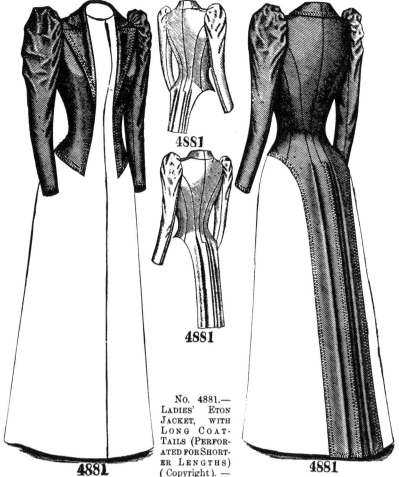

NO. 4881.— LADIES' ETON JACKET, WITH LONG COAT-TAILS (PERFORATED FOR SHORTER LENGTHS) (Copyright). —

This jacket is again represented at figure No. 534 A on page 115. The pattern is in 13 sizes for ladies from 28 to 46 inches, bust measure. To make the garment for a lady of medium size, will require 4⅛ yards of goods 22 inches wide, or 2¼ yards 44 inches wide, or 2⅛ yards 50 inches wide. Price of pattern, 1s. 3d. or 30 cents.

FIGURE NO. 534 A.—LADIES' STREET TOILETTE.—This consists of Ladies' skirt No. 4893 (copyr't), pictured on page 118; Eton jacket No. 4881 (copyr't), on page 114; and blouse No. 4740 (copyr't), on page 96. The skirt pattern is in 9 sizes for ladies from 20 to 36 inches, waist measure, and costs 1s. 6d. or 35 cents. The jacket and blouse patterns are in 13 sizes for ladies from 28 to 46 inches, bust measure, and each costs 1s. 3d. or 30 cents. Of material 22 inches wide for a lady of medium size, the skirt requires 7¼ yards, and the jacket and blouse each 4½ yards.

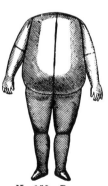

NO. 158.—PATTERN FOR A DOLLS' BODY (DESIGNED FOR SANTA CLAUS AND OTHER CORPULENT DOLLS) (Copyr't). —

This pattern, shown at fig. No. 573 A on page 116, is in 7 sizes for dolls from 12 to 24 ins. tall (with head attached). For goods needed, see page 116. Price, 7d. or 15c.

SET NO. 155.—LADY DOLLS' TRAINED COSTUME (Copyright).—This costume is again pictured at figure No. 570 A on page 118. All rich dress fabrics are adaptable to the mode, and lace, passementerie, ribbon, gimp, etc., will provide suitable garniture. The Set is in 7 sizes for lady dolls from 12 to 24 inches tall. To make the Set for a doll 22 inches tall, will require 2⅛ yards of material 22 inches wide, or 1⅛ yard 44 inches wide. Price of Set, 10d. or 20 cents.

FIGURE NO. 552 A.—MISSES' DERBY CAPE.—This depicts Misses' cape No. 4870 (copyright), which is also shown on page 117. The pattern, which is also adapted to girls' wear, is in 6 sizes from 6 to 16 years of age, and costs 7d. or 15 cents. For a miss of 12 years, it needs 1⅝ yard of material 44, 50 or 54 inches wide.

No. 4890.—Child's Coat (Copyright).—This coat receives further illustration at figure No. 565 A on page 115. The pattern is in 7 sizes for children from 2 to 8 years of age. To make the coat in the combination shown for a child of 5 years, requires 1¾ yard of cloth 54 inches wide, with ⅜ yard of Astrakhan 54 inches wide. Of one material, it needs 4⅝ yards 22 inches wide, or 2⅜ yards 44 inches wide, or 1¾ yard 54 inches wide. Price of pattern, 10d. or 20 cts.

4890

4890

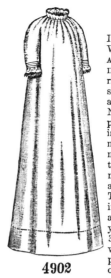

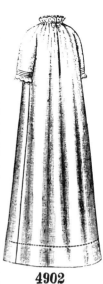

No. 4902.—Infants' Slip, With Body and Sleeves in One (Copyright). — This slip is pictured again at figure No. 567 A on page 111. It is here shown made of fine muslin and trimmed with narrow tucks and edging. The pattern is in one size, and needs 2¼ yards of goods 36 inches wide. Price of pattern, 7d. or 15 cents.

4902

4902

4875

4875

No. 4875.—Girls' Dress (Copyright).—This dress is again pictured at figure No. 559 A on this page. The pattern is in 8 sizes for girls from 5 to 12 years of age. In the combination shown for a girl of 8 years, it needs 2¾ yards of dress goods 40 inches wide, with ¾ yard of velvet 20 inches wide. Of one material, it calls for 5⅝ yards 22 inches wide, or 2¾ yards 44 inches wide. Price of pattern, 1s. or 25 cents.

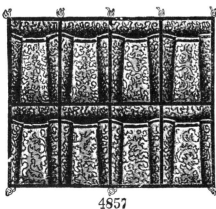

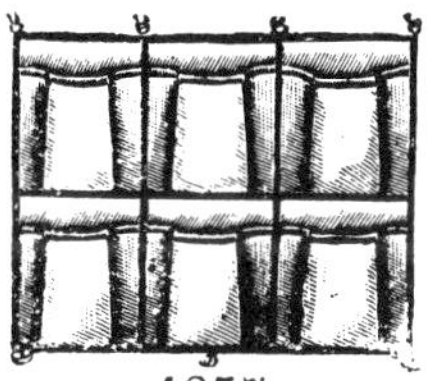

4857

No. 4857.—Shoe-and-Slipper Bag (To be Made with Eight or Fewer Pockets) (Copyr't). —This bag is illustrated made of cretonne and finished with braid. The pattern is in one size, and requires 2⅛ yards of material 20 inches wide, or 1⅝ yard 27 inches wide. If goods 36 inches wide be selected, 1⅛ yard will suffice. Price of pattern, 5d. or 10 cents.

4857

Figure No. 565 A.—Child's Coat.—This illustrates Child's coat No. 4890 (copyright), which is shown made of different materials on page 112 of this publication. The pattern is in 7 sizes for children from 2 to 8 years of age, and costs 10d. or 20 cents. As pictured on page 112 for a child of 5 years, it will need 1¾ yard of cloth and ⅜ yard of Astrakhan each 54 inches wide. Of one material, it calls for 4⅝ yards 22 inches wide, or 2⅜ yards 44 inches wide, or 1¾ yard 54 inches wide.

Figure No. 566 A. — Child's Outdoor Toilette. — This consists of Child's Gretchen cloak No. 4883 (copyright), seen on page 117; and bonnet No. 4846 (copyright), on page 103. The cloak pattern is in 8 sizes for children from ½ to 7 years of age, and costs 10d. or 20 cents. The bonnet pattern is in 8 sizes from ½ to 7 years old, and costs 5d. or 10 cents. For a child of 5 years, the bonnet needs ⅜ yard of goods 20 inches or more wide, with ⅝ yard of silk. Of one material, the bonnet requires ⅝ yard 20 inches or more wide, while the cloak calls for 5½ yards 22 inches wide, or 2⅜ yds. 54 ins. wide.

4896   **4896**

4906

4906   **4906**

No. 4906.—LADIES' COSTUME, WITH A SLIGHT TRAIN (PERFORATED FOR ROUND LENGTH) (Copyr't).—This pattern, also seen at figure No. 544 A on page 116, is in 13 sizes for ladies from 28 to 46 inches, bust measure. For a lady of medium size, it needs 4¾ yards of dress goods 40 inches wide, with 3¼ yards of silk. Of one material, it requires 11¼ yards 22 inches wide, or 5⅝ yards 44 inches wide, or 4⅞ yards 50 ins. wide. Price, 1s. 8d. or 40 cts.

No. 4896.—MISSES' COSTUME (Copyright).—At figure No. 555 A on page 116 this stylish costume may be again observed. The pattern is in 7 sizes for misses from 10 to 16 years of age. In the combination shown for a miss of 12 years, the costume requires 3⅜ yards of dress goods 40 inches wide, and 1⅛ yard of velvet. Of one material, it needs 6⅜ yards 22 inches wide, or 3⅜ yards 44 inches wide. Price of pattern, 1s. 6d. or 35 cents.

4911   **4911**

No. 4911.—LITTLE GIRLS' DRESS (Copyr't).—This pattern, also pictured at figure No. 564 A on page 111, is in 8 sizes for little girls from 2 to 9 years old. As shown for a girl of 5 years, it needs 2 yards of plaid dress goods 40 inches wide, with 1⅝ yard of plain silk. Of one material, it requires 4⅞ yards 22 inches wide, or 2½ yards 44 inches wide. Price of pattern, 10d. or 20 cents.

4886

No. 4886.— LADIES' DOU- BLE-BREASTED COAT (IN THREE-QUAR- TER LENGTH) (Copyright).— By referring to figure No. 524 A on page 112, this coat may be seen made of rever- sible coating. Fancy coating was here cho- sen for its de-

4886   **4886**

velopment, with machine-stitching for a completion. The pattern is in 13 sizes for ladies from 28 to 46 inches, bust measure. To make the garment for a lady of medium size, will require 7½ yards of material 22 inches wide, or 3¾ yards 44 inches wide, or 3⅛ yards 54 inches wide. Price of pattern, 1s. 6d. or 35 cents.

128

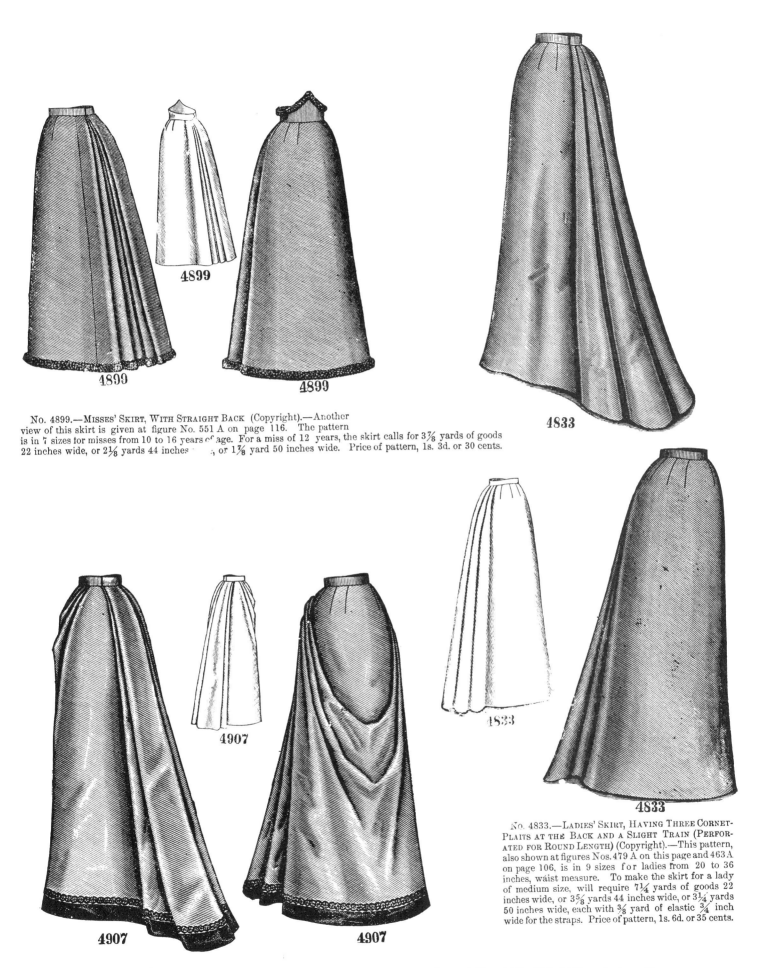

4899

4899

4899

4833

No. 4899.—Misses' Skirt, With Straight Back (Copyright).—Another view of this skirt is given at figure No. 551 A on page 116. The pattern is in 7 sizes for misses from 10 to 16 years of age. For a miss of 12 years, the skirt calls for 3⅞ yards of goods 22 inches wide, or 2⅛ yards 44 inches ·   ·, or 1⅞ yard 50 inches wide. Price of pattern, 1s. 3d. or 30 cents.

4907

4833

4907

4907

4833

No. 4833.—Ladies' Skirt, Having Three Cornet-Plaits at the Back and a Slight Train (Perforated for Round Length) (Copyright).—This pattern, also shown at figures Nos. 479 A on this page and 463 A on page 106, is in 9 sizes for ladies from 20 to 36 inches, waist measure. To make the skirt for a lady of medium size, will require 7¼ yards of goods 22 inches wide, or 3⅝ yards 44 inches wide, or 3¼ yards 50 inches wide, each with ⅜ yard of elastic ¾ inch wide for the straps. Price of pattern, 1s. 6d. or 35 cents.

No. 4907.—Ladies' Draped Skirt, with a Slight Train (Perforated for Round Length) (Copyright).—This skirt is again shown at figure No. 520 A on page 117. The pattern is in 9 sizes for ladies from 20 to 36 inches, waist measure. For a lady of medium size, it requires 6⅛ yards of material 22 inches wide, or 3⅛ yards 44 inches wide, or 3 yards 50 inches wide. Price of pattern, 1s. 6d. or 35 cents.

FIGURE NO. 573 A.—SANTA CLAUS' COSTUME.—This consists of Santa Claus' costume, No. 159 (copyright), also shown on page 113; and Dolls' body No. 158 (copyright), on page 114. Flannel or some similar variety of woollen goods will usually be chosen for developing the costume, and muslin or Canton flannel will be used for the body, with cotton for the stuffing. The costume pattern is in 7 sizes for dolls from 12 to 24 inches in height and costs 10d. or 20 cents. The body is in 7 sizes for dolls from 12 to 24 inches tall (with head attached), and costs 7d. or 15 cents. To make the costume for a doll 22 inches tall, will require 1½ yard of material 27 inches wide, or ¾ yard of goods 54 inches wide. The body calls for ½ yard of material 36 inches wide, with a piece of white leather measuring 6 x 10¼ inches.

FIGURE NO. 572 A.—BABY DOLLS' TOILETTE.—This consists of the dress and sack included in Set No. 157 (copyright), which also includes a skirt and is pictured in full on page 118. White nainsook was here employed for the dress, with white lace for trimming; and flannel was chosen for the sack, with ribbon for a decoration. The Set is in 7 sizes for baby dolls from 12 to 24 inches in height, and costs 10d. or 20 cents. As shown on page 118 for a baby doll 22 inches tall, the dress calls for 1¾ yard of lawn 36 inches wide, with ⅛ yard of fancy tucking 27 inches wide; the skirt requires 1⅝ yard of cambric 36 inches wide, and the sack, ⅜ yard of cashmere 40 inches wide.

4900

4900

NO. 4900.—GIRLS RUSSIAN COAT (Copyright).—By referring to figure No. 557 A on page 114, this comfortable coat may be observed differently developed. It is here pictured made of rough-faced cloth and trimmed with buttons and Astrakhan. The pattern is in 8 sizes for girls from 5 to 12 years of age. For a girl of 8 years, it needs 4¾ yards of goods 22 inches wide, or 2¾ yards 44 inches wide, or 2¼ yards 54 inches wide. Price of pattern, 1s. or 25 cents.

FIGURE NO. 528 A.—LADIES' EMPIRE COSTUME.—This illustrates Ladies' costume No. 4887 (copyr't), also seen on page 113. The pattern is in 13 sizes for ladies from 28 to 46 inches, bust measure, and costs 1s. 8d. or 40 cents. Of one material for a lady of medium size, it calls for 12 yards 22 inches wide, or 5⅝ yards 50 inches wide.

FIGURE NO. 559 A.—GIRLS' DRESS.—
This illustrates Girls' dress No. 4875 (copyright), which is again depicted on this
page. The pattern is in 8 sizes for girls
from 5 to 12 years of age, and costs 1s. or
25 cents. As shown elsewhere on this
page for a girl of 8 years, the dress needs
2¾ yards of dress goods 40 inches wide,
with ¾ yard of velvet 20 inches wide.
Of one material, it calls for 5⅝ yards 22
inches wide, or 2¾ yards 44 inches wide.

FIGURE NO. 556 A.—MISSES' VICTORIA CAPE.—This illustrates
Misses' cape No. 4908 (copyright), which is shown differently developed on page 112. The pattern is also cut in sizes for girls;
it is in 7 sizes from 4 to 16 years of age, and costs 10d. or 20
cents. To make the garment of one material for a miss of 12 years,
requires 2½ yards 44 inches wide, or 2⅜ yards 54 inches wide.

FIGURE NO. 550 A.—MISSES' RUSSIAN
TOILETTE.—This consists of Misses' Russian
coat No. 4904 (copyr't), also shown on page
113; and corselet Princess skirt with suspenders No. 4725 (copyright), on page 91.
Both patterns are in 7 sizes for misses from
10 to 16 years old, and each costs 1s. 3d. or
30 cents. For a miss of 12 years, the coat
requires 4⅞ yards of material 22 inches
wide, or 2¾ yards 44 inches wide, or 2⅛
yards 54 inches wide; the skirt needs 3¾
yards 22 inches wide, or 2⅞ yards 30
inches wide, or 2¼ yards 44 inches
wide, or 1⅞ yard 50 inches wide.

FIGURE NO. 551 A.—MISSES' HOUSE
TOILETTE.—This consists of Misses' skirt
No. 4899 (copyright), shown again on page
115; and blouse-waist No. 4223 (copyright),
seen on page 52. Both patterns are in 7
sizes for misses from 10 to 16 years of age:
the skirt costing 1s. 3d. or 30 cents; and
the blouse-waist, 1s. or 25 cents. Of one
material for a miss of 12 years, the toilette
requires 7¾ yards 22 inches wide; the
skirt and waist each calling for 3⅞
yards. If goods 44 inches wide be selected, then 4¼ yards will prove amply
sufficient, each garment needing 2⅛ yards.

4889 **4889**

No. 4889.—Girls' Dress (Copyright).—This pattern, also shown at figure No. 561 A on page 111, is in 8 sizes for girls from 5 to 12 years old. In the combination shown for a girl of 8 years, it will require 2½ yards of dark and ½ yard of light cloth 50 inches wide. Of one material, it needs 5⅝ yards 22 inches wide, or 4⅜ yards 30 inches wide, or 3 yards 44 inches wide. Price of pattern, 1s. or 25 cents.

Figure No. 532 A.—Ladies' Short-Waist Empire Gown.—This depicts Ladies' Empire gown No. 4912 (copyright), which is again illustrated on page 112. Black China silk is here shown in the gown, and white silk mull black moiré ribbon furnish tasteful garniture. The pattern is in 13 sizes for ladies from 28 to 46 inches, bust measure, and costs 1s. 6d. or 35 cents. Of one material for a lady of medium size, the gown calls for 10½ yards 22 inches wide, or 8½ yards 27 inches wide, or 5⅞ yards 44 inches wide.

4885

4885 **4885**

No. 4885.—Ladies' Greek Dress (Also Known as the Penelope Gown), with a Slight Train (Perforated for Round Length) (Copyright).—This pattern is in 13 sizes for ladies from 28 to 46 inches, bust measure. To make the garment for a lady of medium size, will require 12¼ yards of goods 22 inches wide, or 10 yards 27 inches wide, or 6⅛ yards 44 inches wide. Price of pattern, 1s. 8d. or 40 cents.

FIGURE No. 519 A.—LADIES' RUSSIAN COSTUME.—
This represents Ladies' costume No. 4905 (copyright),
shown again on this page. In the present instance, serge,
velvet and plaid Surah are charmingly associated in the
construction of the costume, the velvet and Surah also
constituting the decoration. The pattern is in 13 sizes
for ladies from 28 to 46 inches, bust measure, and costs
1s. 8d. or 40 cents. Of one material for a lady of
medium size, it needs 13⅛ yards 22 inches wide, or 6¾
yards 44 inches wide, or 5⅞ yards 50 inches wide.

FIGURE No. 520 A.—LADIES' MOURNING TOILETTE.—This consists of Ladies' skirt No. 4907 (copyright), shown on page 113;
and basque No. 4898 (copyright), pictured on page 114. The skirt
pattern is in 9 sizes for ladies from 20 to 36 inches, waist measure,
and costs 1s. 6d. or 35 cents. The basque pattern is in 13 sizes for
ladies from 28 to 46 inches, bust measure, and costs 1s. 3d. or 30
cents. Of one material for a lady of medium size, the toilette requires 10⅛ yards 22 inches wide; the skirt calling for 6⅛ yards,
and the basque for 4 yards. Of 44-inch-wide goods, 5⅛ yards will
suffice, the skirt needing 3⅛ yards and the basque, 2 yards

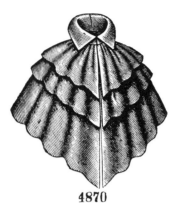

4870

4870

4870

4870

No. 4870.—Misses' and Girls' Cape (Known as the Derby Cape) (Copyright).—This stylish cape is pictured made of cloth, with ribbon ties bowed at the throat, at figure No. 552 A on page 115. Cardinal cloth was chosen for making the garment in the present instance. The cape may be made up with one, two or three capes, and the corners of the collars may be square or round. The pattern is in 6 sizes from 6 to 16 years of age. To make the garment for a miss of 12 years, will require $1\frac{5}{8}$ yard of material either 44, 50 or 54 inches wide. Price of pattern, 7d. or 15 cents.

4883

No. 4883. — Child's Gret-chen Cloak (Copyright).— This stylish lit-tle cloak is again depicted at fig-ure No. 566 A on page 115. The pattern is in 8 sizes for children from $\frac{1}{2}$ to 7 years of age. To make the garment for a child of 5 years, will require $5\frac{1}{2}$ yards of material 22 inches wide, or $2\frac{3}{4}$ yards 44 inches wide, or $2\frac{3}{8}$ yards 54 inches wide. Price of pattern, 10d. or 20 cents.

4883

4883

Figure No. 523 A.—Ladies' Outdoor Toilette.—This consists of Ladies' coat No. 4862 (copy't), again shown on page 114; and skirt No. 4893 (copyright), seen on page 118. The coat pattern is in 3 sizes for ladies from 28 to 46 inches, bust measure; the skirt pattern is in 9 sizes for ladies from 20 to 36 inches, waist measure, and each costs 1s. 6d. or 35 cents. For quantities of material needed, see pages 114 a.

No. 4882. — Girls' Cloak, with Removable Cape (Copyright).—At figure No. 558 A on page 112 this cloak is shown made of different materials. It is here pictured developed in Russian-green cloth. The pattern is in 7 sizes for girls from 3 to 9 years old. To make the cloak for a girl of 8 years, needs 7⅛ yards of material 22 inches wide, or 3½ yards 44 inches wide, or 2⅞ yards 54 inches wide. Price of pattern, 1s. or 25 cents.

4882

4903

4903　**4903**

No. 4903.—Ladies' Costume, with a Slight Train (Perforated for Round Length) (Copyright).—Another stylish development of this costume may be observed at figure No. 543 A on page 118. The pattern is in 13 sizes for ladies from 28 to 46 inches, bust measure. For a lady of medium size, it needs 10½ yards of goods 22 inches wide, or 5⅛ yards 44 inches wide, or 4¾ yards 50 inches wide. Price of pattern, 1s. 8d. or 40 cents.

Figure No. 545 A.—Ladies' Promenade Toilette.— This consists of Ladies' cape No. 4869 (copyright), which may be again seen by referring to page 111; and skirt No. 4877 (copyright), also shown on page 116 of this publication. The cape pattern is in 10 sizes for ladies from 28 to 46 inches, bust measure, and costs 10d. or 20 cents. The skirt pattern is in 9 sizes for ladies from 20 to 36 inches, waist measure, and costs 1s. 6d. or 35 cents. For a lady of medium size, the toilette requires 6 yards of material 44 inches wide; the cape calling for 2 yards, and the skirt for 4 yards. Of goods 50 inches wide, 5⅝ yards will prove sufficient: the cape needing 2 yards; and the skirt, 3⅝ yards.

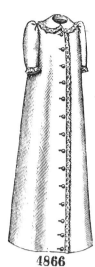

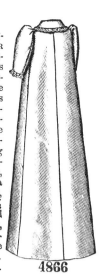

No. 4866.—IN-
FANTS' WRAPPER
(Copyright).—An-
other view of this
wrapper is por-
trayed at figure
No. 568 A on this
page. White flan-
nel was here cho-
sen for making the
wrapper, and em-
broidered edging
trims it. The pat-
tern is in one size,
and, to make a
wrapper like it,
will require 2⅞
yards of material
27 inches wide,
or 1⅞ yard 36 in-
ches wide. Price
of pattern, 10d.
or 20 cents.

4866

4866

FIGURE NO. 553 A.—MISSES' COAT-BASQUE.—This represents Misses'
coat-basque No. 4879 (copyright), which may be again seen on page
113. A stylish combination of serge, velvet and India silk is shown
in this instance. The pattern is in 7 sizes for misses from 10 to 16
years of age, and costs 1s. or 25 cents. To make the garment for a
miss of 12 years, requires 3⅝ yards of material 22 inches wide, or 1⅞
yard 44 inches wide. In the combination shown on page 113, it needs
1⅜ yard of serge 44 inches wide, with 1 yard of silk 20 inches wide

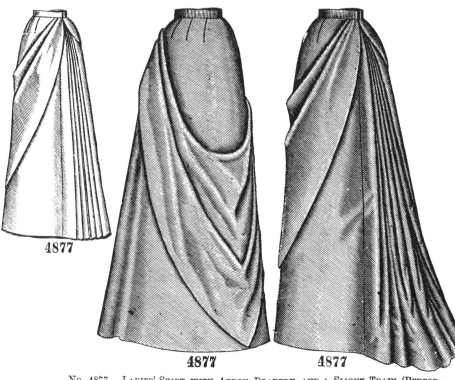

4877

4877

4877

FIGURE NO. 543 A.—LADIES' VISITING COSTUME.—
This illustrates Ladies' costume No. 4903 (copyright),
shown again on page 117. The pattern is in 3 sizes for
ladies from 28 to 46 inches, bust measure, and costs 1s.
8d. or 40 cents. For a lady of medium size, the costume
requires 10½ yards of material 22 inches wide, or 5⅛
yard 22 inches wide, or 4¾ yards 50 inches wide.

NO. 4877.—LADIES' SKIRT, WITH APRON-DRAPERY, AND A SLIGHT TRAIN (PERFOR-
ATED FOR ROUND LENGTH) (Copyright).—This skirt may be again seen at figure No.
545 A on page 118. The pattern is in 9 sizes for ladies from 20 to 36 inches, waist
measure. For a lady of medium size, it requires 8⅝ yards of material 22 inches wide,
or 4 yards 44 inches wide, or 3⅝ yards 50 inches wide. Price of pattern, 1s. 6d. or 35 cts.

4865

4865

No. 4865.— Misses' Flannel Petticoat, with Yoke.—Flannel was chosen for this skirt, with cambric for the yoke. The pattern is in 9 sizes for misses from 8 to 16 years of age. For a miss of 12 years, the garment requires $2\frac{3}{4}$ yards of flannel 27 inches wide, and $\frac{5}{8}$ yard of cambric 36 inches wide. Of one material, it calls for $3\frac{1}{4}$ yards 27 inches wide, or $2\frac{1}{2}$ yards 36 inches wide. Price of pattern, 10d. or 20 cents.

4884

4884

4884

4884

No. 4884.— Ladies' Skirt, having Two Cornet-Plaits at the Back, and a Short Train (Perforated for Round Length) (Copyright).—The pattern of this fashionable skirt, which is pictured developed in dark cloth, is in 9 sizes for ladies from 20 to 36 inches, waist measure. Cloth, cheviot, serge, camel's-hair, Henrietta cloth and cashmere will develop nicely by the mode. To make the skirt for a lady of medium size, will require $6\frac{1}{8}$ yards of goods 22 inches wide, or $3\frac{1}{8}$ yards 44 inches wide, or $2\frac{7}{8}$ yards 50 inches wide. In each instance $\frac{1}{2}$ yard of elastic 1 inch wide will be needed for straps. Price of pattern, 1s. 6d. or 35 cents.

4893

4893

4893

No. 4893.—Ladies' Skirt, With a Straight Back, and a Slight Train (Perforated for Round Length) (Copyright).—Different views of this skirt are given at figures Nos. 524 A, 534 A and 523 A on pages 112, 115 and 117. In the present instance the skirt is shown made of dark-green cloth and trimmed with black Astrakhan. The pattern is in 9 sizes for ladies from 20 to 36 inches, waist measure. To make the skirt for a lady of medium size, will require $7\frac{1}{4}$ yards of material 22 inches wide, or $3\frac{1}{4}$ yards 44 inches wide, or 3 yards 50 inches wide. Price of pattern, 1s. 6d. or 35 cents.

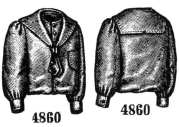

4860   **4860**

No. 4860.—Little Boys' Sailor Blouse (Copyright). — This little blouse is again shown at figure No. 569 A on this page. The pattern is in 7 sizes for little boys from 2 to 8 years of age. To make the garment for a boy of 5 years, calls for 2 yards of goods 27 inches wide, or ⅞ yard 54 inches wide. Price of pattern, 10d. or 20 cents.

Figure No. 568 A.—Infants' Wrapper.—This shows Infants' wrapper No. 4866 (copyright), pictured again elsewhere on this page. The pattern is in one size, and costs 10d. or 20 cents. To make the wrapper needs 2⅞ yards of goods 27 inches wide, or 1⅞ yard 36 inches wide.

Figure No. 527 A. — Ladies' Empire Costume.—This shows a partial back view of Ladies' costume No. 4887 (copyright), seen on page 113. A full front view is shown at figure No. 528 A on page 116. The pattern is in 13 sizes for ladies from 28 to 46 ins., bust meas., and costs 1s. 8d. or 40 cents. For goods needed see page 113.

Figure No. 563 A.—Little Girls' Dress.—This illustrates Little Girls' dress No. 4874 (copyright), which may be again seen by referring to page 116 of this publication. The pattern is in 7 sizes for little girls from 2 to 8 years of age, and costs 10d. or 20 cents. To make the dress as represented on page 116 for a girl of 5 years, will call for 2⅝ yards of serge 40 inches wide, with ⅜ yard of velvet 20 inches wide. Of one material, it will need 5¼ yards 22 inches wide, or 2⅝ yards 44 inches wide.

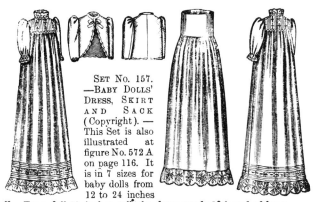

Set No. 157.—Baby Dolls' Dress, Skirt and Sack (Copyright). — This Set is also illustrated at figure No. 572 A on page 116. It is in 7 sizes for baby dolls from 12 to 24 inches tall. For a doll 22 inches tall, the dress needs 1¾ yard of lawn 36 inches wide, and ⅛ yard of fancy tucking 27 inches wide; the skirt requires 1⅝ yard of cambric 36 inches wide, and the sack, ⅜ yard of cashmere 40 inches wide. Price of Set, 10d. or 20 cents.

Figure No. 569 A. — Little Boys' Sailor Suit.—This consists of Little Boys' sailor blouse No. 4860 (copyright), which is again portrayed on this page; kilt skirt No. 4718 (copyright), also seen on page 94 of this issue; and cap No. 3033, pictured on page 66. The blouse pattern is in 7 sizes for little boys from 2 to 8 years of age, and costs 10d. or 20 cents. The skirt pattern is in 6 sizes for little boys from 2 to 7 years old, and costs 7d. or 15 cents. The cap pattern is in 7 sizes from 6 to 6¾, hat sizes, or from 19¼ to 21½ inches, head measures, and costs 5d. or 10 cents. For quantities of materials, see pages mentioned.

Figure No. 570 A. — Lady Dolls' Trained Costume.—This is Lady Dolls' Set No. 155 (copyright), shown on page 115. The Set is in 7 sizes for lady dolls from 12 to 24 inches in height, and costs 10d. or 20 cents. For a doll 22 inches tall, it requires 2⅛ yards of material 22 inches wide, or 1⅛ yard 44 inches wide.